```
853.1 Boc Hol
Hollander.
Boccaccio's last fiction,
 "Il Corbaccio."
```

**The Lorette Wilmot Library
Nazareth College of Rochester**

Boccaccio's Last Fiction

Boccaccio's Last Fiction "Il Corbaccio"

ROBERT HOLLANDER

UNIVERSITY OF PENNSYLVANIA PRESS *upp* Philadelphia

University of Pennsylvania Press
MIDDLE AGES SERIES
Edited by EDWARD PETERS
Henry Charles Lea Professor
of Medieval History
University of Pennsylvania

A complete listing of the books in this series
appears at the back of this volume

Copyright © 1988 by the University of Pennsylvania Press
All rights reserved
Printed in the United States of America

Library of Congress Cataloging-in-Publication Data

Hollander, Robert.
    Boccaccio's last fiction, Il Corbaccio / Robert Hollander.
      p.   cm.—(University of Pennsylvania Press Middle Ages series)
    Bibliography: p.
    Includes index.
    ISBN 0-8122-8127-6
    1. Boccaccio, Giovanni, 1313–1375. Corbaccio. I. Title.
II. Title: Corbaccio. III. Series.
PQ4270.C73H65   1988
853'.1—dc19   88-14393
                                                       CIP

CONTENTS

Boccaccio's Last Fiction: *Il Corbaccio*   1

Notes   45

Appendix 1: Texts in the *Corbaccio* Reflecting Passages in Dante   59

Appendix 2: The Proem of the *Corbaccio:* Sources and Analogues   72

Appendix 3: A Partial Census of Some Critical Views Concerning Various Problems in the *Corbaccio*   76

Appendix 4: The *Remedia Amoris* and the *Proemio* of the *Decameron*   78

Bibliography   81

Index   85

BOCCACCIO'S LAST FICTION:
IL CORBACCIO

Il est bien plus aisé d'accuser l'un sexe, que d'excuser l'autre. C'est ce qu'on dict: le fourgon se moque de la poele.
(Montaigne, *Essais*, III, 5)

*B*OCCACCIO's final work in vernacular fiction has been for the most part an embarrassment, even to its admirers. It is almost universally understood as running counter to the spirit of the preceding masterwork, the *Decameron*. And few who are drawn to the study of this apparently shrill misogynist outburst find it possible to argue that it has, to borrow again from Montaigne, "come from the same shop." Yet, whether it was written in 1354–55 or in 1365–66 (a problem of some current interest which will detain us later), the fact remains that, for all our difficulty in giving secure dates to Boccaccio's works, no one who has studied the Boccaccian *oeuvre* with care has suggested that *Decameron* and *Corbaccio* are not "neighbors." While I will later argue for the traditional dating of the work (1354–55), which makes it a "next-door neighbor" to the hundred tales, even a later dating of the text would allow that, in whatever ways, the *Corbaccio* might profitably be dealt with as a work which manifests a continuation of the themes, subjects, and techniques of the *Decameron*, that it might in fact be in relation to the latter in the role of an "afterword" or *conclusione*.[1] This essay is meant to call into question the more customary interpretations of the last prose fiction of the Florentine master. After presenting my views concerning the structure and development of the text itself, including a consideration of its relationship to its most evident precursor in the *Decameron* (VIII, 7), I will then attempt to open a path for several revisionary understandings, which may briefly be described as follows: 1) the Boccaccian narrator is, as usual, to be conceived as foolish; 2) the text is a companion piece to the *Decameron*, not a later recantation of its values; 3) its title reflects its simultaneously satiric and parodic nature; 4) the work is to be conceived as an Ovidian (and thus ironic) *retractio*, as a playful "confessio amantis"; 5) its evident and frequent recourse to the texts of Dante serves to underline its distance from rather than its dependence upon the moral strategies of the Dantean original. In short, I shall argue that the *Corbaccio* is, as has only recently been suggested (Barricelli [1975]), a literary joke.[2]

It is fair to say that little attention has been paid to the care with which Boccaccio has organized and articulated the relation among the parts of the *Corbaccio*. One is tempted to assert that most readers have not thought of its subdivisions at all, preferring to consider the work an unswerving and unpartitioned autobiographical outburst against the female sex. In any case, and perhaps understandably, since the text is presented without clear marginal or rubrical indications of its divisions, no one has paid public heed to the elaborate and balanced organizing principles of the work. The following tabular representations will offer some immediate sense of exactly how carefully structured the work is (the numbers in parentheses refer to Nurmela's numeration of the parts of the text).

(1–5)	*proemio*	\multicolumn{2}{l}{thanksgiving, desire to be of use to others, and invocation of divine assistance in writing the book}
(6–53)	situational frame	\multicolumn{2}{l}{Boethian consultation and sleep}
(54–131)	"little *Inferno*"	\multicolumn{2}{l}{1) dream vision of Hell 2) dialogue with spirit-guide}
(132–177)	the lover's tale	autobiography:	1) his *innamoramento* 2) the fatal letter
(178–290)	the guide's speech	particular: general: general: particular:	1) the scholar's fault 2) *contra feminas* 3) *pro hominibus* 4) the scholar's fault
(291–512)	the guide's tale	biography:	1) his wife's behavior 2) her response to his letter

(513–554)	"mini-*Purgatorio*"	1) dialogue with spirit-guide
		2) dream vision of Purgatory
(555–559)	situational frame	awakening and Boethian consultation
(560–562)	*conclusione*	thanksgiving, hope to be of use to others, that God will punish widow

The chiasmic organization of the work may thus be displayed as follows:

(1) narrator *in propria persona*
   (2) narrative: his situation
      (3) dream vision (Hell)
         (4) lover's autobiography
            (5) guide's oration
         (6) guide's biography of wife
      (7) dream vision (Purgatory)
   (8) narrative: his situation
(9) narrator *in propria persona*

That the work is effectively in nine parts is interesting for its resonances with Boccaccio's own earlier work, which is also in nine parts (*Filostrato*, *Elegia di madonna Fiammetta*), as well as for its probable reflection of Dante's favorite number. What seems to me most interesting, however, in the formal arrangement of the parts of the *Corbaccio* is the effect the presence of so highly wrought a design—a perfectly balanced chiasmic structure—has (or should have) on its reader.[3] The misogynist diatribe, which most readers—often apparently characterizing the work from a memory of earlier unhappy encounters with the text—take as its virtually sole concern, occurs at its center, in its fifth and sixth parts. It issues, significantly, from the mouth of the guide, not even from that of the putative "Boccaccio" who is telling us all this. Everything about the arrangement calls out for us to think of artifice, of a fictive narrative, as Nykrog (1984) has recently tried to tell us. And when we read the text sequentially, Boccaccio's strategies also seem more apparent than we have usually allowed ourselves to perceive (and here I point an accusing finger not only at others, but also at my younger self). With the exception of Barricelli and, to a certain degree, Cassell (1974, 1975), students of Boccaccio who have dealt with the work have remained convinced that it must be taken "seriously."[4] It is probably worth taking the time to review the text's contents before we consider more closely its possible meanings. And while such an undertaking asks for patience on the reader's part, the condition of the discussion of the *Corbaccio* which we currently possess may be fairly characterized as urging upon us a return to the text itself, rather than reliance on our more general recollections of its contents.

It is useful to imagine that we are mutually reading the *Corbaccio* for the first time, innocent of any knowledge about it or about its author, if perhaps possessing some acquaintance with earlier literature and some knowledge of its own literary conventions. In short, it would be helpful to take on the role of a contemporary reader of the text, one who has happened upon it in a friend's study and picks it up for perhaps two hours of reading. What are our likely reactions to this text if we come to it without being convinced that we know what it means to tell us before we begin reading?

1. The narrator's introduction (1–5). The proem seems to ask us to take the work very seriously indeed. We hear of benefits received that ought to be acknowledged with gratitude, of grace obtained from God by the intercession of Mary. This the narrator will now record, with God's illuminating aid, so that "per me quello si scriva che onore e gloria sia del suo santissimo nome e utilità e consolazione dell'anime di coloro li quali per avventura ciò leggeranno" [that I may write that which will be the honor and glory of His most Holy Name, and that this work may be of use and consolation to the souls of those who may chance to read it] (5). Hearing this much, what do we imagine the rest will reveal? Surely we confront a writer who wants to tell us of a soul-searing experience, one that nearly brought him to his death, perhaps, and that at the very least was marked by such sinful behavior on his part that we must rejoice along with him at the great and generous forgiveness of God. And while I would argue that even the *proemio*, like its predecessor in the *Decameron*, is far more "literary" in its gestures than has generally been supposed, it would not be proper to make that case in this context, which is posited on a more innocent reading.[5] The narrator to whom we listen, given the nature of the words which he utters, seems almost necessarily to be taken as speaking in seriousness and in truth. Hearing his words, we have as yet no reason to interpret his speech in any other way, nor any indication of the need to assume an ironic distance from him.

2. *Boethian consolation and sleep (6–53).* As the *pars executiva* of the *Corbaccio* begins, we immediately learn the cause of the narrator's trouble: "gli accidenti del carnale amore" [the vicissitudes of carnal love] (6). These, then, will be his subject. Alone in his room, he reaches the following conclusion: ". . . giudicai che senza alcuna mia colpa io fossi fieramente trattato male da colei, la quale io mattamente per mia singulare donna eletta avea, e la quale io più assai che la mia propria vita amava e oltre ad ogni altra onorava e reveriva" [I concluded that through no fault of mine I had been cruelly ill-treated by her whom I had chosen in my madness as my special lady and whom I honored and revered above all others and loved far more than life itself] (7). The speaker, while he does admit to some foolishness in loving this woman, immediately puts the entire blame for his unhappiness upon her. We will soon have grounds on which to question the validity of his view of the woman's culpability. At this point in our reading, however, all we can assert is that the question is an open one—our unhappy lover may be speaking the truth. Yet surely we are warned by the conclusion of this period that he is a flowery speaker, one who does not so much pay heed to the need to express truth as he yields to being tempted toward rhetorical exaggeration. His love for his lady is protested overmuch, or so our awareness of similar confessions is likely to suggest to us. However, if he blames his lady's cruelty, he simultaneously admits his own foolishness ("bestialità"—9). Then, in a passage which mirrors the judgmental nature of the one we have just examined in §7, he records the crucial moment in his subsequent judgment: ". . . estimai che molto men grave dovesse essere la morte che cotal vita, e quella con sommo disidero cominciai a chiamare" [I decided that Death must be far easier to bear than such a life; and I began to cry out to him with the greatest longing] (9). The resulting battle of conflicting thoughts concerning suicide is resolved only by the ratiocination provided by his personified "thought," which comes to convince him to return to a desire for life.[6]

The clearly Boethian framework of the ensuing monologue (13–46) offers us our first indication that the narrator's initial complaint is to be considered from another point of view than has as yet been made available. This projection of his inner voice, which he now believes to have been sent to him by heavenly light ("credo da celeste lume mandato"—12), is a fourteenth-century "municipal" version of Boethian wisdom.

His opening sally, "Deh stolto!" {You silly fool!} (13), puts us on guard.[7] If we are about to hear unvarnished home truths, delivered in hopes of putting a foolish lover back on the track, we hear them from a provocative source, one whose very diction undercuts the seriousness of the moment. His message, on the other hand, seems "orthodox" enough. Where the narrator has previously held his lady blameworthy, the "thought" puts the fault solely upon him: "tu, non ella, ti se' della tua noia cagione" [you, not she, are the cause of your torment] (17). And he continues by paraphrasing and then commenting upon the narrator's logical procedures in the following condemnatory way: "«Ella, conoscendo che io l'amo, dovrebbe amar me; il che non faccendo, m'è di questa noia cagione; e con questo mi ci mena e con questo mi ci tiene.» Questa non è ragione che abbia alcun valore: forse che non le piaci tu. Come vuoi tu che alcuno ami quello che non gli piace?" ["She should love me, knowing that I love her; and by not doing so, she is the cause of this grief of mine; with this she leads me here and with this she holds me." This is not a valid reason at all. Perhaps she finds you unpleasing. How do you expect anyone to love a person whom she does not find attractive?] (19–21). The unanswerable argument receives no answer.

The narrator's *noia* (and we should remember the importance of that word as it works its way from the *Proemio* through the rest of the *Decameron*, joining the twinned phenomena of plague and carnal appetite in its first appearances)[8] is self-caused. The "thought" expounds, in a low-mimetic version of scholastic argument, the logical reasons which stand against his intention to do away with himself (25–46): if you love her and she loves you, your death will cause her pain; if she hates you, your misery will give her pleasure. Thus it is best to give over mad desire for sexual pleasure: "tuo folle amore" (42—see *Paradiso* VIII, 2), "questo tuo folle appetito" (43).

All this is conventional wisdom of a most familiar Boethian strain. In place of the narrator's first version of the "love affair," we now have a better one. However, even the *pensiero* seems to realize that, in order to convince his auditor to go on living, he must supply a positive reason for doing so. The conventions of his monologue lead us to expect a conventional conclusion, urging his auditor to turn aside from the vanities of such behavior to seek a better being in philosophy or religion, or at least in contented abnegation among those who have also been freed from the pangs of love. The conclusion of this first oration of the *Corbaccio*, however, is quite different from what we have been led to expect: If the narrator goes on living, no one can say with certitude that he will take pleasure from his lady; but if he dies he will certainly not achieve the joys of revenge (". . . ogni speranza di vendetta od altra letizia di cosa che qui rimanga, fugge, nel morire, a ciascuno" [all hope of revenge, or any other joy in things which remain here below, flees everyone at his death]—45). Therefore, he should choose to live on, thereby making her unhappy by his very existence (44–46). It is a surprising resolution. In place of the concupiscible appetite, the narrator is enjoined to put himself under the sway of the irascible. If nearly everything else in the oration is conventional, with the exception of its comic tone, its ending is far from being so. Instead, it offers the narrator exactly the wrong advice, urging him to continue his passionate feelings in another and complementary form, exchanging hatred for lust. As I shall later argue, *vendetta* is perhaps the key word of the *Corbaccio*. We have seen it introduced in this passage. Our basic interpretation of the work depends on whether or not we consider the narrator's desire for vengeance as being presented as a praiseworthy form of behavior.[9]

The effect of this admonition is enormous and immediate. As we begin the second segment of this section of the work, we hear the following gratified outburst from the narrator in response to the advice he has just been given:

> Maravigliosa cosa è quella della divina consolazione nelle menti de' mortali: questo pensiero, siccome io arbitro, dal piissimo Padre de' lumi mandato, quasi dagli occhi della mente ogni oscurità levatami, in tanto la vista di quegli aguzzò e rendé chiara, che a me stesso manifestamente scoprendosi il mio errore, non solamente, riguardandolo, me ne vergognai, ma da compunzione debita mosso, ne lagrimai e me medesimo biasimai forte, e da meno che io non arbitrava d'essere mi reputai.
>
> [Divine consolation in the minds of mortals is a wondrous thing. This thought, sent, I believe, by the most holy Father of Lights, took away almost all the darkness from the eyes of my mind and at the same time sharpened and cleared their vision; so that finding my error so obvious, not only did I feel ashamed as I looked upon it, but, moved by due repentance, I wept about it bitterly, reproved myself, and felt less self-esteem than before]. (47)

Again, let us imagine that we are reading these words for the first time. Do we not seem to be hearing a *recusatio* of the most serious sort? Is not this man cured of his disease? Had the "thought" not finished his oration as he did, had not the promise of *vendetta* been the culminating point in his argument, and were not the narrator to spend the rest of his literary effort in search of this revenge, we might think—as so many readers have thought—that we are dealing with a genuine Christian conversion to the good, even one which might mirror such an occurrence in Boccaccio's own life. Boccaccio, playful as always, allows us to read past the promise of *vendetta* as though it were not there (there is, in fact, no reference to it in the lengthy expression of thanksgiving which we have just examined). He will exploit the power of this prolonged desire for revenge as the work progresses, for we will see that it is the sole motivation for all else that the narrator finally thinks and does, although it will take some time to resurface.

Indeed, the second Boethian scene of this part of the *Corbaccio* is also without reference to vengeance. Instead, we see the refreshed narrator, his face serene, leave his room to find a group of friends with whom he withdraws to a familiar pleasant surrounding for discourse of a philosophical kind. They speak of changeful Fortune (49), of abiding natural laws (50), and of Divinity, whose nature exceeds human comprehension (51). After a day spent with friends in such lofty pursuits, the narrator returns, *consolato*, to his chamber, where he recalls the day's conversations with pleasure and finally finds the ease of sleep (53).

If the *Corbaccio* had concluded here, we would be tempted to read it as most readers have read the work as a whole, believing that Boccaccio had left us a brief, Boethian homiletic treatment concerning the best ways to deal with the pangs of unrequited love for an unworthy woman. But the *pensiero*, who reveals to the lover the true nature of his love for the woman (in some respects resembling the "thought" [*pensero*] in *Vita Nuova* XLI, who reveals something of the true nature of Beatrice to her lover), has made available a single possibility for the furtherance of the plot. Instead of aiming for a philosophic acceptance of things as they are and for thoughts of a better directed future course, the narrator will be bent on vengeance. If he cannot get sexual pleasure, he will at least get even. We might reflect that the *pensiero* is, after all, a part of the narrator's own psyche, not an external agent of reform—despite what his own claims for its divine provenance may insist. The sheepish lover may be won back to life only by the hope for vengeance, no matter that only the Lord should be relied on to repay ("Non vosmetipsos defendentes charissimi, sed date locum irae. Scriptum est enim: Mihi vindicta: ego retribuam, dicit Dominus" [Dearly beloved, avenge not yourselves, but rather give place unto wrath: for it is written, Vengeance is mine; I will repay, saith the Lord]—Romans 12:19).

3. Dream vision and dialogue (54–131). The narrator's dream will occupy over nine-tenths of the work (§§54–554 in Nurmela's edition, or all but 8 of its 105 pages) and is divided into five parts, as I have already indicated. Its introduction shows how intent its author is upon warning his readers to be alert to the changes he has wrought upon our expectations. The narrator has been made healthy—or so it would appear—by the combined result of the intervention of his "thought" and the philosophical musings enjoyed with his friends. If he is now to dream (and *there*'s the rub), we expect the vision presented to him to be the further agent of his recovery, reinforcing the message he has already had so clearly presented for his amelioration. Yet the dream will cause him to return to his dilemma, as his own words suggest: ". . . non parendo alla mia nemica fortuna che le bastassero le 'ngiurie fattemi nel mio vegghiare, ancora dormendo s'ingegnò di noiarmi" [my enemy Fortune, believing that she had not done me sufficient injuries during my waking hours, contrived to harm me even as I slept] (54). His complaint against Fortune, whom he has only recently presented as being expectably unstable (49), reveals how little Boethian advancement he has in fact accomplished.[10] The dream offers a return to *noia*, a word, as I have suggested, that brings with it the context of the *Decameron*'s conjoining of plague and carnal love. If the narrator was "consoled" after his conversations with himself and with his friends, the dream, apparently, has the function of making him once again a sick man, precisely by reminding him of the *noia* he has suffered from the widow's disdain.

The first segment of this part of the dream vision is pure narrative (54–73) and contains the most evidently Dantean elements of the *Corbaccio*, as has often been noted.[11] This exercise in pastiche is put to amusing service. The dream landscape, which begins with visions of delight, ends with unmistakably Dantean reminiscences of Hell ("una solitudine diserta, aspra e fiera, piena di salvatiche piante, di pruni e di bronchi" [a desolate wilderness, rough and harsh, rankly overgrown with trees, thorns, and brambles]—61), where our narrator hears bestial cries that similarly derive from Dante ("mugghi, urli e strida" [roars, howls, and shrieks]—63).[12] And, as the spirit-guide in the dream—Boccaccio's version of Dante's Virgil—will point out, what seems so foul is in reality what the narrator has always taken for fair: carnal affection for the opposite sex. This figure, perhaps the most realized presence in Boccaccio's cunning fiction, is an after-the-fact rigid moralist, a former lover himself who will prove almost pitiless in his castigation of present lovers.[13]

The second segment of this first part of the dream vision (73–131) is devoted nearly entirely to dialogue.[14] In the second section of the *Corbaccio* the *pensiero* had indeed spoken, delivering himself of a lengthy speech (13–46), but there was no verbal interaction between speaker and listener, as befitted that situation, in which a character was listening to his own inner voice. Now, however, what had been only first-person narrative, from opening prayer to ensuing relation of event to following dream, becomes a mixture of narrative and Dantesque otherworldly dialogue, which, paradoxically, soon begins to seem both more immediate and more "realistic" than what had preceded.

The guide's first word to his pupil is the (playfully unreported) name of the narrator (leaving us to supply the "Giovanni" if we are so minded), when he calls out to him, "per lo mio proprio nome chiamando" (73).[15] The act of naming establishes links between *magister* and pupil, between both of them and their similarly unnamed city ("la comune patria"—78).[16] We learn gradually of the tie that binds these two men, first only that the elder of them was once wrathful against the younger, but that his wrath is now turned (as is fitting in a purging spirit) to charity (82). That news comes in company with the notice that the speaker is no longer among the living, information which fills the narrator with the dread apprehension that he is addressing a ghost and which reminds us that we are witnessing an otherworldly scene. That the relation between them is their mutual woman, one who has often cuckolded her husband but who avoided at least one act of posthumous sexual betrayal because she did not respond to the advances of the middle-aged scholar, sets the encounter in a low-comedic atmosphere that dominates the rest of the work.

Our protagonists share a common negative attribute: neither of them is particularly successful with women. The first purpose of this guide is to reassure his charge; his second, to educate him concerning the nature of his desires for sexual pleasure. Both tasks are completed by the conclusion of this section of dialogue. The narrator comes to understand that the "hell" of lust punished is no more than the eventual condition of lust indulged. The "laberinto d'amore" (93), which had at first seemed to be the opposite of the "dilettevole e bel sentiero" [delightful and beautiful path] (54) which had led him there, turns out to be only its logically necessary destination: "Questa misera valle è quella corte che tu chiami «d'Amore» e quelle bestie che tu di' che udite hai e odi mugghiare sono i miseri, de' quali tu se' uno, dal fallace amore inretiti" [This wretched valley is what you call "the Court of Love"; and these beasts, which you say you heard and hear growling, are the wretches—of whom you are one—who have been caught in the net of false love] (124).

4. The narrator's tale of his beloved (132-177). The next fictional mode assumed by the text is that of autobiography.[17] This section of the *Corbaccio* is also in two parts, or movements. In the first, the narrator rehearses his *innamoramento* with his guide's widow. A male relative of the departed spirit had praised his widow to the narrator (135), with the inevitable result: the scholar decides to fall in love (141). He seeks out the widow. Once again, his good opinion of her is entirely due to the opinions of another, this time a lady who claims that the widow's mourning dress becomes her (145). The narrator still does not know the identity of his beloved and does not do so until the helpful lady points her out to other female onlookers ("La terza, che siede in su quella panca" [The third one seated on that bench]—147). It is enough, this first, literarily unpromising sight of his beloved. He burns with the fire of love (150). Her appearance, he claims, gives him hopes for future bliss (151). It is important to note that, even in the narrator's own version of this "primal scene" in any medieval love story, there is absolutely no indication of the widow's interest in him. (As we shall see, if the widow is nothing else, she is constant precisely in her aversion to the narrator.)

At this point, the ghostly guide intervenes (154) to set the questions which will be answered in the second part of the narrator's love story, asking his pupil to explain how he revealed his affection to the widow and whether she ever encouraged him (certainly a valid question in light of the scant information we have previously been offered). The narrator confesses (and the scene is indeed reminiscent of a confessional encounter between priest and sinner) to having written a letter expressing his affection, to which the widow responded with limping epistolary verses alluding to the migration of souls between lovers and seeking to know his identity. The trap had been set. Not even the literary pretensions of the widow's letter are sufficient to cause the lover's retreat. He writes again, as she had requested. And therein, as he tells us at some length (167–175), lay his woe. The lady wanted him further to reveal himself only in order to be able to mock him; in fact, her own letter had been composed not by her but by her lover, the two of them conspiring to enjoy his discomfort. The guide's question which produces this response is worth pondering: "Se più avanti in questo amore non è stato, che cagione t'induceva, il dì trapassato, con tante lagrime e con tanto dolore sì ferventemente per questo a disiderare di morire?" [If there were no further developments in this love affair, what induced you when the day was over to desire death so fervently for this—with so many tears and so much grief?] (166) If we have not thought so previously, can we now avoid understanding that the lover's problem is not a broken heart but spite? He had wanted to kill himself from shame. The guide's response summarizes what we have learned in this section (177): ". . . come tu t'innamorasti e di cui, e il perché e la cagione della tua disperazione . . ." [how you became enamored, and of whom, and the reason and cause of your despair . . .].

5. *The guide's misogynist diatribe (178–290)*. The last three questions (how, with whom, and why did the narrator fall in love) are used to organize the central section of the work. The husband's outburst, presented as a single, developed rhetorical unit, an *oratio contra feminas*, is what most readers of the *Corbaccio* take to be the central point of the work, considering it as reflecting Boccaccio's own latter-day view of womankind. It is divided into four parts, the first of which is a brief presentation of the charge against the lover himself (179–194), and is thus concerned with the particular and not the general case, for he is portrayed as the source of his own incorrect behavior. Both his age (179–187) and his studies (188–194) should have served to quell such a desire.

This first segment ends with a peroration declaiming the blindness of love (193–194). The lengthy presentation (195–273) of the general case begins with the repeated assertion that the narrator's studies should have revealed the nature of women to him. Since they obviously did not, the guide makes up for this lack with a full-scale oration *contra feminas*. This begins by claiming that women are like privies, to which one resorts out of necessity in order to deposit a necessary discharge but otherwise strives to avoid (201), and rapidly becomes still more wildly vituperative.[18] The major topics which he chooses to address are as follows: women's use of cosmetics (207–208); their desire to assume *signoria* over their husbands as quickly as possible (209–221);[19] their urge to take lovers once their husbands are made subject (222–233); their suspicious and wrathful nature (234–239); their avarice (240–244); their flightiness, with their only constant desire being lust itself (245–246); the vain wishes and vain knowledge revealed by their incessant garrulity (247–269). We are spared a recounting of still other defects when the guide tells the narrator that this would take too long and that enough has already been told to convince him of the flaws of womankind (270–273).

To this oration on a general theme is joined a second, a mad forerunner of Pico della Mirandola's oration on the dignity of man (274–278). The *oratio pro hominibus* would have it that males, made (unlike women) in the image of God, are born to lordship over women, not to be subject to them. The fourth part of the oration returns to the particular.[20] Scholars are themselves superior to other men (279–280). How then, the guide wants to know, can the narrator desire so vile a woman (281–282)? Instead, he should consort with the Muses—so superior in beauty to *malvage femmine*—in deserted places, not seek pleasure under widows' cloaks (282–290). And it is with this piece of wisdom that the guide pauses before entering another avenue of attack.

6. The widower's revenge: Biography of a wife (291–512). Moving from oratory to biography, the guide warms to his task with relish and at length. Where his first assault upon the heart and mind of the amatory scholar has primarily assumed the form of oratorical presentation of a *quaestio*, the worth of women, his concluding argument is less an oration *contra feminas* than it is spectacularly an argument *ad feminam*. A widower himself, he tells us he first knew his new and monstrous wife, herself a widow, when their marriage was arranged by relatives and friends (292).[21] He then proceeds to reel off a list of her faults. As we shall see, its contents closely correspond to those which were produced in the *contra feminas* portion of his oration (207–269).

As soon as they were married, his new wife assumed *signoria* over him, making their home life more full of quarrels than the strife-torn city itself (293–301). The guide then details the result of her avaricious desire to gain control of his wealth: her expenditures on vestments and cosmetics to make herself more attractive (302–337). If asked, she would have insisted that her cosmetic extravagances (which the guide has displayed with venomous and compendious detail) were committed for his sake; in fact, she employed them in order to attract other men, of whom there were many, including one to whom she gave his goods (350) and with whom she shared her sexual favors (338–375). Next, he turns to her vain wishes to be admired for her noble lineage and to the empty folly revealed in her insistent and incessant talk (376–385).

The preceding four segments of his description correspond to charges we have heard about women in general. Now the guide marshals his culminating evidence against his former wife: Since, he says, doctors must sometimes prescribe harsh medicines, he will now display her physical attributes as they actually are. Undressing her, at least in words, he describes first her undecorated face, then her pendulous breasts, her belly, her huge vaginal aperture, and finally her anus (386–422). The prosecution rests its case and now makes its final plea to the jury (423–452): In light of the above, the scholar-lover must acknowledge that his opinion of her virtues was wrongly based (was she steadfast? no, she delighted in his sudden death, brought on by the stress caused by her behavior, bought a house [in which her "paternosters" are French romances] near a church in order to seem pious, but actually to find paramours in that church).[22] In the course of this penultimate harangue, the guide refers to the scholar's main rival, the "second Absalom" (443). He tells the narrator that, although his spirit is offended by his wife's infidelity with this younger lover, he will one day have his revenge (*vendetta*),[23] since he himself had previously cuckolded "Absalom," whose son by his lawful wife is in fact the guide's (444).

While no further persuasions would seem necessary, the guide cannot resist a concluding thrust (453–512), thus adding a second element to this "biography" of his wife. It is perfectly calculated to be the most telling of all. He informs the narrator that spirits in Purgatory are at certain times vouchsafed visits to their loved ones and friends on earth (454). As a result, it happened that he was back in his own house, "tirato da una cotale caritevole affezione la quale non solamente gli amici, ma ancora i nimici ci fa amare" [drawn by a certain charitable affection, which makes us love not only our friends but also our enemies] (455).[24] And there he sees his wife in bed with "Absalom," witnesses their mocking of the nar-

Boccaccio's Last Fiction

rator's first letter, their plans for his further vilification (456–465). Had the narrator known of all this then as certainly as he knows it now, the guide suggests, he surely would have hanged himself (468). How could he have loved such a creature? His mind should have convinced him of her unworthiness (476–493). If not, then his natural advantages (maleness, physical comeliness at least as great as hers, relative youth) should have helped him to control himself. And if her noble lineage made him feel inferior, her behavior reveals that she is not noble in any true sense at all (501–511). And with that final demonstration the guide falls silent, awaiting the narrator's response (512).

7. *The narrator's penitence (513–554)*. In chiasmic parallel with its corresponding section of the work (the third), in which an otherworldly dialogue is preceded by an otherworldly experience, this one begins with such a dialogue (514–544). The narrator has come round, has utterly changed his opinion of his beloved, but now fears that, after such sinfulness, he must despair of pardon (514–517). God's mercy, he is told, may extend even unto him if he is truly contrite and truly makes amends (518–520). The narrator proclaims his contrition and wants to know exactly how he can atone for his sin (521). The guide informs him (522–530): "Ciò che tu hai amato ti conviene avere in odio . . .; voglio che della offesa fattati da lei tu prenda vendetta; la quale ad un' ora sarà a te e a lei salutifera" [What you have loved you must hate . . .; I wish you to avenge the offense she has done to you, for it is something which will bring salvation to both of you at the same time] (523, 526).[25] As for the particular form this penitent hatred should take, a scholar like him,

> eziandio mentendo, sa cui gli piace tanto famoso e sì glorioso rendere negli orecchi degli uomini, che chiunque di quel cotale niuna cosa ascolta, lui e per virtù e per meriti sopra i cieli estiman tenere le piante de' piedi; e così in contrario, quantunque virtuoso, quantunque valoroso, quantunque da bene stato sia uno che nella vostra ira caggia, con parole che degne paiono di fede nel profondo di ninferno il tuffate e nascondete.
>
> [can render even by fiction whom he pleases so famous and so glorious to the ears of men, that whoever hears anything of that person, considers him to have the very soles of his feet above the heavens both because of his virtue and his merits; and so, on the contrary, however virtuous, however worthy and upstanding a person may be who enrages you, with words which seem believable, you cast and hide him in the depths of Hell] (527).[26]

It is thus that the guide "commissions" *Il Corbaccio*. The narrator is quick to accept the charge. As long as skillfully crafted words maintain their power, he says, "a niuno mio successore lascerò a far delle ingiurie ricevute da me vendetta, solo che tanto tempo mi sia prestato che io possa o concordare le rime o distendere le prose" [I will leave none of my successors to avenge the outrage I have received, if only I am granted enough time either to tune my rhymes or to draft my prose] (532).[27] The word *vendetta* has now passed from the *pensiero* (45) to the guide (444, 526) to the narrator himself. He at last has hold of his purpose. Continuing, he says that he will leave the *vendetta* of deeds ("la quale i più degli uomini giudicherebbono che fosse da far co' ferri" [which most men would judge should be taken with the sword]—533) to God. But then all writers think the pen is mightier than the sword—especially *their* pen. And his disclaimer in no way indicates that he hopes his literary effort will help to bring the widow to self-knowledge and thus perhaps eventual salvation, a possibility three times held out by the guide in his last speech. On the contrary, he hopes that God will indeed punish her.

This section is rounded off by a statement of the narrator's desire to know why the guide was chosen in heaven to come to his aid when they never knew one another (537). The guide replies that souls in Purgatory are moved by disinterested charity, and that, in any case, he knew the details of the case better than anyone (538–541). The narrator's response is to ask what he can do for his benefactor (542),[28] who responds that, since he has no one to pray for him, he would appreciate the narrator's paying to have a few masses said in order to lessen his torment in Purgatory (543).[29]

The concluding part of this section, balancing the Infernal descent of the third section of the *Corbaccio*, presents a Purgatorial ascent. The narrator feels the weight of sin lifted from his back and follows the guide along a shining path upward (545–550). The view from the mountaintop reveals both a lovely landscape and the hellish hole which represents earthly love and wherein he began. He turns to offer thanks to his guide only to find him gone,[30] and his dream ended as well (551–554).

8. Awakening and Boethian consultation (555–559). Awakening from his dream, the narrator decides that it was a truthful one—as later consultation would affirm (555). He leaves the *misera valle* to rejoin his friends, who confirm his interpretation of the dream; he decides to cease loving the widow, within a few days regaining his lost *libertà* (556–558).[31] His final remark in this section shows little concern for the soul of the widow: "E senza fallo, se tempo mi fia conceduto, io spero sì con parole gastigare colei, che vilissima cosa essendo, altrui di schernire co' suoi amanti presume, che mai lettera non mostrerà che mandata le sia, che della mia e del mio nome con dolere e con vergogna non si ricordi" [Without fail, if time be granted to me, I hope with my words so to chastise that woman—who, though she is a contemptible thing, presumes to mock others with her lovers—that she will never show a letter sent to her without recalling mine and my name with grief and shame] (559).[32] The entire energy of the former lover is now bent just as fiercely on hate as it was on love.[33]

9. The narrator's conclusion: "Go, little book" (560–562). In his envoy the narrator, reversing the intention expressed in almost all of the concluding passages in Boccaccio's earlier vernacular works,[34] wants his book to avoid his beloved, not to find and inflame her:

> Ma sopra ogni cosa ti guarda di non venire nelle mani delle malvage femmine, e massimamente di colei che ogni demonio di malvagità trapassa e che della presente tua fatica è stata cagione; per ciò che tu saresti là mal ricevuta; ed ella è da pugnere con più aguto stimolo che tu non porti teco. Il quale, concedendolo Colui che d'ogni grazia è donatore, tosto a pugnerla non temendo le si farà incontro.
>
> [But above all, see that you do not come into the hands of evil women, especially into those of her who surpasses every demon in wickedness and who has been the cause of your present toil, since you would be ill received. She is to be stung by a sharper goad than you bear with you; this will advance upon her swiftly and fearlessly to wound her, if the Giver of all Grace grants it.] 561–562 [35]

The narrator is clearly referring to §533, where, in addition to his own literary vengeance, he hopes for the *vendetta di Dio* to strike his former lady. He has, once again, forgotten entirely about the guide's advice that his correction may bring the widow to self-knowledge and, eventually, to salvation. Instead, all the narrator really desires is revenge (and, if Cassell is correct, he does so with a similarly "stony" envoy of Dante's in mind).[36] It is worthy of note that Dante's poem ("Così nel mio parlar voglio esser aspro") ends with the very word which has had such an important role in revealing the motives of the narrator of the *Corbaccio*:

> Canzon, vattene dritto a quella donna
>   che m'ha ferito il core e che m'invola
>   quello ond'io ho più gola,
>   a dàlle per lo cor d'una saetta;
>   ché bell'onor s'acquista in far vendetta.

[My song, get yourself straight to that lady who has wounded my heart and who robs me of what I most hunger for, and shoot an arrow through her heart; for fair honor is won by taking revenge.]

The *Corbaccio* is not a work that is out of control, as so many have thought. It is a work about a man who is out of control.

THE SCHOLAR AND THE WIDOW: *DECAMERON* VIII, 7

The *novella* concerning the scholar and the widow told by Pampinea—the oldest of the ladies in the *Decameron*'s *brigata*[37]—has long been treated as an "autobiographical" companion piece to the *Corbaccio*.[38] More recently, students of Boccaccio have distanced themselves from such positivistic views. However, until very recently we find the interpreters of the *novella* unanimous in taking it "straight." Until Millicent Marcus published her essay (1984), the universal view had been that Boccaccio either identified completely with the scholar or at least essentially approved of the vengeance his character perpetrates upon the teasing widow. Marcus's argument, in my opinion, constitutes the first major step toward a better appreciation of the significance of the *novella*. She first argues that Boccaccio's desire to include misogynist treatises among the compendium of genres that constitutes the *Decameron* is controlled, not the result of some personal grudge; second, that the text explores critically the anti-female behavior of thwarted lovers even more urgently than it criticizes the flighty behavior of sensual women.

Decameron VIII, 7, the longest *novella* in the collection, is narrated by Pampinea, whose rubric for the tale (3) is probably the single most significant cause of its usual interpretation. She tells her companions that they have heard many tales during this Day in which those who play tricks (*beffe*) on others escape unscathed;[39] in hers, a "just retribution" will be seen visited upon a Florentine woman. Her conclusion (149) reinforces this interpretation: She warns the ladies to be cautious when they play tricks, particularly when they play them on scholars. Assuredly, such a view of the narrative, which makes it conform to the model of the *beffatore beffato*, is an adequate reading of one part of the narrative. The foolish and nasty widow gets at least as much as she deserves. But what of the scholar? As is so frequently the case in the *Decameron*, it is the part of the *novella* which escapes from the reductive constraint of the apparently controlling rubrics, whether these are imposed by the author, by the queen of the Day, or by the narrator, that is the most engaging and challenging.

Unlike the antagonist of the *Corbaccio*, the widow of the *novella* has a name: Elena. She is the only character in the *Decameron* to bear this name. Helen of Troy is frequently referred to in the earlier works (several times, for instance, in each of the following: *Filocolo, Filostrato, Teseida, Amorosa Visione, Comedia delle ninfe*), and we can hardly believe that Boccaccio did not think of her as he named his Elena, "una giovane del corpo bella e d'animo altiera e di legnaggio assai gentile" [a young woman of comely shape, lofty mind, and most noble lineage] (4).[40] If her would-be lover, Rinieri, is not named "Paris," at least he has just come home from there.[41] Helen of Florence, recently widowed, does not want to marry (4), preferring to keep company with her unnamed young paramour. Rinieri, seeing her at a *festa* in her widow's black, immediately falls in love with her.[42] The course of the beautifully managed narrative is familiar and needs no retelling: boy woos girl, girl plays trick on boy (who nearly dies from spending a night imprisoned in a courtyard in the winter snow), boy gets even with girl (who nearly dies from spending a day imprisoned on a tower in the summer sun). That the widow makes love to her employment is beyond question. Like the Fiammetta of the *Elegia*, she is prideful, lecherous, and foolish. Abandoned by her young lover, she puts herself into Rinieri's trap when she believes he possesses necromantic skills,[43] learned in Paris, to bring that lover back to her by casting a spell (46–55). The lady is characterized as "più innamorata che savia" [more loving than wise] (55), and we have come to realize that, where at first she seemed a woman possessed of considerable poise and intelligence, regardless of the worthiness of her pursuits, she now seems out of control, as was he, supposedly "il savio scolare," when he first became enamored of her (10). Now that he has gained control of the situation, *he* seems to have the same abilities and self-possession we had previously seen in her.

The crucial scene of the *novella* (66–67) occurs when Rinieri, observing his *innamorata* pass naked before him in the night, undergoes the war between pity (*compassione* for the woman in the plight into which his machinations have put her) and eros (his erection and desire to move forward out of the darkness to ravish her). Either a humane response or a "natural" one would have ended the *beffa* at this point, and in such a way as to illustrate the exemplary instruction insisted on by Pampinea: "una giusta retribuzione a una nostra cittadina renduta" [just retribution visited upon a fellow townswoman of ours] (3). But another instinct arises in him, dispelling both "la compassione e il carnale appetito" [compassion and sexual appetite] (68): the desire for revenge (". . . nella memoria tornandosi chi egli era e qual fosse la 'ngiuria ricevuta . . ." [. . . when he remembered who he was {a scholar!} and the nature of his slight . . .]—68). The rest of the *novella* (and we have not quite reached its midpoint here) is devoted to his achievement of that revenge. At the lady's subsequent pleas Rinieri betrays two emotions: "piacere della vendetta la quale più che altra cosa disiderata avea, e noia sentiva movendolo la umanità sua a compassion della misera" [pleasure in the revenge which he had desired more than anything else, while, at the same time, he felt distress moving his humanity toward compassion for the poor creature] (80).[44] The text continues: "ma pur, non potendo la umanità vincere la fierezza dell'appetito . . ." [but then, his humanity unable to overcome the fierceness of his appetite . . .] (80).

Rinieri's concupiscible appetite has turned into an irascible one, exactly as will later be the case for the narrator of the *Corbaccio*. And it is at precisely this point that narrative ceases in favor of an inserted misogynist harangue (81–100), occupying, just as in the *Corbaccio*, the central section of the work, here between the two main narrative sections. The first part of this outburst (81–91) is entirely personal, detailing Rinieri's complaint against the widow. She, in response, begs for mercy, even offering him the favors which he had so ardently desired in the first place—the "revenge" that most men would be likely to find most appropriate (". . . e te solo avere per amadore e per signore" [. . . and to have you alone as my lover and my lord]—94). Would you, she continues, see me die before "gli occhi tuoi, a' quali, se tu bugiardo non eri come se' diventato, già piacqui cotanto" [your eyes, to which, if you were not the liar you have become, I was so pleasing] (95)? As Branca's note to the passage points out (p. 1438), her phrase recollects *Purgatorio* I, 85: "Marzia piacque tanto a li occhi miei" [Marcia was so pleasing in my eyes]. The scholar has become another Cato (shortly before the widow has referred to his

Catonic "severa rigidezza" [rigid severity] (89), casting his too sensual woman from him.[45]

The quotation carries its effect into the second part of the misogynistic diatribe, when the scholar becomes boastful, proclaiming that he would have been capable of trapping the widow in any number of ways in the service of his revenge, and then becomes a first version of the cuckolded husband and misogynist orator of the *Corbaccio*.[46] Since he is a scholar, he could, he insists, have chosen to write things of her so terrible that she would have torn her eyes out rather than look on herself any longer (100)—the ancient wounding, cursing nature of satire is clearly alluded to here. And now he addresses *all* women, not the widow alone, with the plural *voi* (102–105). He offers, in this conclusion of his speech, a traditional old man's attack on women for preferring youthful lovers. Indeed, he speaks as though he himself were such an older man.[47] When we reflect that he is in fact young ("un giovane chiamato Rinieri"—5), that in the finale of his peroration he apparently lies, claiming that he now has a paramour far superior to her (106),[48] we probably ought to realize that he is utterly out of control, has temporarily become a maddened old man. This is familiar territory for a reader of the *Corbaccio*. How interpreters have considered the passage to represent Baccaccio's own views is beyond comprehension, especially since the young scholar's strange behavior calls such attention to itself.

The aesthetic structure of the *novella* is, as many have noticed, perfectly balanced. What has not been understood nearly so well by commentators (with the near exception of Marcus) is the way in which its moral content is equally distributed as well. Rather than observing a battle in which an offended party justly triumphs over the offender, we witness a struggle between two victims of uncontrolled appetites, one for sexual pleasure, another for the displaced form of the same, sexual revenge, in which both characters may be observed in a harsh light.[49] The sins of lust and pride are clearly at work in these characters, along with anger in Rinieri. But what both of them most dramatically present for our inspection is the trace of envy, in particular the desire to see those who are happy made unhappy. The widow's joys in the sufferings of the scholar, and his still greater joy in hers, are both probably to be understood as reflecting the presence of this sinful disposition.

In this connection, I would like to point out that in this *novella*

Boccaccio's Last Fiction

Boccaccio has frequent recourse to *Purgatorio* XIV, the terrace of Envy. When Elena gains control over Rinieri, we are told that she "il tenne gran tempo in pastura" [kept him long at pasture] (14), an evident allusion to *Purgatorio* XIV, 42, "che par che Circe li avesse in pastura" [that it seems that Circe held them at pasture], words describing the inhabitants of the valley of the Arno, "li abitator de la misera valle" (XIV, 41)—a phrase which is probably remembered in the *misera valle* of the *Corbaccio* (66, 556). The sunburned widow is described as having "il corpo suo tutto *riarso* del sole" [her body completely burned by the sun] (124), an evident citation of *Purgatorio* XIV, 82–84. Guido del Duca speaks: "Fu il sangue mio d'invidia sì *riarso*, / che se veduto avesse uom farsi lieto, / visto m'avresti di livore sparso" [My blood was so inflamed by envy that, when I saw someone filled with joy, you would have seen me suffused by lividness].[50] And perhaps a still more telling revisitation of the terrace of Envy occurs at the very end of the seventh Day. I have already alluded to Lauretta's putting down her own desire for "revenge" on Dioneo by making the *beffe* played by husbands on wives the subject for the next round of *novelle*. Her decision to make her Day sexually neutral sets the tone for our better understanding of the war between men and women, which so largely offers itself for display in the *Decameron* (and particularly in this portion of the work). To clarify her motives in *not* biting back at Dioneo's sexually focused satirical intent (*contra feminas*), while confessing that, as a woman, she would like to, she says, "e, se non fosse che io non voglio mostrare d'essere di schiatta di can botolo che incontanente si vuol vindicare, io direi che domane si dovesse ragionare delle beffe che gli uomini fanno alle lor mogli" [and, were it not that I do not wish to seem to be descended from ravening hounds that instantly desire to take revenge, I would say that tomorrow we should speak of the tricks which men play on their wives] (VII, Conc., 3). Her temperate and healing gesture reminds us that *vendetta* is not, for all its intense pleasure, the most humane course. Her phrase "schiatta di can botolo" recalls *Purgatorio* XIV, 46, the valley of the Arno again, where the denizens of Arezzo are "botoli."[51]

It seems absolutely clear to me that both these tales of love rejected and the ensuing desire for revenge are to be read at a distance.[52] Yet, until very recently, those who thought that Boccaccio identified with these scholarly seekers of *vendetta* have been untroubled by such doubts, despite

Boccaccio's Last Fiction

some fairly evident warning signs in the texts. Rinieri, the narrator of the *Corbaccio*, and the latter's guide and mentor are all better regarded as male hysterics than as lance bearers in an imagined Boccaccian war against women. The protagonist of Boccaccio's *Elegia di madonna Fiammetta* has seemed to some a fourteenth-century precursor of Emma Bovary;[53] perhaps the two middle-aged Florentines of the *Corbaccio* may be thought of as looking forward to the same author's Bouvard and Pécuchet.

If the *Corbaccio* is, as I believe it is, a companion piece to the *Decameron*, what purpose did Boccaccio see it as serving? Such questions are difficult and hazardous, but nonetheless worth confronting. In order to approach them, I propose to take up the several questions which I indicated as being essential to my own approach in my introductory remarks.

THE BOCCACCIAN NARRATOR

In my *Boccaccio's Two Venuses* I devoted some pages to the *Corbaccio*.[54] While I am pleased to note, looking back over those pages, that I thrice hedged my position (pp. 21, 28, 120), allowing that an ironic reading of the narrator's view of what he recounts is a possible interpretation, my own response to the *Corbaccio* at that time was essentially, even pugnaciously, "orthodox." I must confess to the interested reader that I would handle my tactics in developing a general approach to all of Boccaccio's *opere minori in volgare* differently were I to write that book over again. The one text, however, and as is evident by now, about which I have most emphatically changed my mind is the *Corbaccio*. When, some years ago, I told my colleague Victoria Kirkham, perhaps the most adroit of the moralizing readers of Boccaccio's fictions, of this change in my view of Boccaccio's last *fabula*, she seemed disconcerted. I was letting the side down, as it were.

Let me try to address the problem which faces those of us who attempt to deal with Boccaccio's fictions as being inextricably bound to the moral concerns of European writing extending from St. Augustine's time to Dante's. I remain firmly convinced that, even in his first Latin literary efforts, and surely by the time of composition of the *Caccia di Diana*,

Boccaccio sees himself as inheriting this literary tradition. What has changed in my approach is that I now believe that, throughout his career as maker of vernacular fiction, Boccaccio is more interested in studying the phenomenon of human behavior than in attempting to shape morals. Thus, while I do not budge at all from the position advanced throughout *Boccaccio's Two Venuses* that even the younger Boccaccio is completely conversant with the traditional moral readings of such diverse phenomena as the "religion of love" or of such discrete icons as the lustful Dido or the figure of Fortuna, what I now propose is that traditional moral readings of these texts are as much at risk as the more conventional post-Romantic view, which simply disregards the "medieval" quality of Boccaccio's literary vision.[55]

To translate these thoughts into perhaps dangerously simple terms, I would not consider Boccaccio (as I consider Chaucer) an ironic medieval writer rather than a pre-modern enthusiast of whatever persuasion may be proposed for him—and there have been several. If, in his Latin works, Boccaccio strikes the all-too-familiar pose of the ardent humanist, his fictions are not marked by such grandiose gesturing. Even at his classicizing worst (the *Amorosa Visione* may be the obvious example to pick on), he manages to be amusing and light-hearted, playing games with his erudition even as he asserts it. In the world of Boccaccian fable, scholars may seem every bit as foolish as businessmen.

One of the most difficult characteristics of Boccaccio's work is found in its deliberate evocation in its reader of expectations of autobiographical revelations. Since we tend to come to Boccaccio from Dante, we perhaps understandably enjoy entertaining the thought that the Boccaccian narrator speaks *in propria persona*.[56] The issue is more complicated than those of us who insist on the fictitiousness of Boccaccio's fiction are eager to confirm. It is convenient for us to dismiss the "autobiographers" (for example, Crescini and De Gubernatis) because of their rather naive assumptions about the absolute relations between fictional events and their "autobiographical" counterparts. However, it may not be eventually just that we do so. I think it is fair to say that Boccaccio, like Dante, created his fictions out of the fabric of his life. I think it is also fair to say that we possess neither the knowledge, the resources to create new knowledge, nor perhaps the patience, had we the first two, to unravel the elaborate skein of autobiographical reference that runs throughout the works. On the other hand, it does seem totally clear that, in his use of elements of his own autobiography or "pseudo-autobiography" (and we are surely hard-pressed if we must determine where these two kinds of self-presentation might be separated), Boccaccio is not slavishly telling us his story so much as developing an authorial persona. It is thus, in my opinion, that we are never other than at risk if we attempt to pin him down to a single identity as we find this reflected in the fictions. The voice of the Boccaccian narrator is distinguished by being always unreliable or, at best, enigmatic. Nor am I certain that we should be entirely comfortable with the generally accepted notion that the Boccaccio of the Latin works speaks unequivocally. But that is a notion that I leave aside in this discussion.

As I look back to my own enthusiastic "discovery" of the hidden schemes of the younger Boccaccio, I can see why I was so excited by what I began to see in the *opere minori* some dozen years ago. Here were texts which hardly any other critics had perceived to have significant points of contact with the "orthodox" Christian literary conventions of their age. I continue to believe that these are present in such a way as to create the central issues which demand to be confronted in these texts, if I am less certain of the way in which we are being asked to resolve our responses to them. I would now be a good deal more circumspect concerning the happy "Christian" endings of *Filocolo*, *Comedia delle ninfe fiorentine*, and *Ninfale fiesolano*.[57] They are, perhaps, too good to be true, leading the reader to wonder whether they might not be meant to be perceived as having been imposed upon resistant material. On the other hand, I would feel less revisionary zeal in reconsidering the works which deal ironically with their subjects, allowing us to see the distance separating what Boccaccian characters call "love" and what we should probably consider vanity.

What my earlier study may contribute to our understanding of all of Boccaccio's fiction is a sense of the ironic distance which always characterizes the relation between Boccaccio and his narrator. The one rule I suggest we can apply with confidence to *all* of Boccaccio's fiction is the following: Boccaccio never speaks openly *in propria persona*. The presence of a narrative frame in all his fictions is not only a secure sign of his authorship, but also affords his narrators the necessary space to deport themselves as characters, and to give us the opportunity to see that they and their author may not share many attitudes, if they do share similar interests. What appalls me, as I reconsider my findings in *Boccaccio's Two Venuses*, is that it was not more obvious to me (and I had Barricelli's clear statement, as well as Cassell's precautions, to guide me) that the narrator of the *Corbaccio* is no exception. Since it was I who first proposed that the Boccaccian narrator is not to be trusted, why did I make a single exception? I can see why, if I am not pleased by what I see: I wanted an "orthodox" *Corbaccio* as a reflection of all the *opere minori*, and just about everyone else in Boccaccio studies granted me a "serious" Boccaccio as author of the *Corbaccio*. The *Corbaccio* was the one Boccaccian work about which everyone else would tend to agree with me. Since I was arguing against the generally held view of Boccaccio's fictions, that fact itself should perhaps have been fair warning.

THE DATE OF THE *CORBACCIO*

The *Corbaccio*, by and large (at least until recently), has not in itself been a problematic text. The problem caused by this apparently non-problematic vituperative assault upon the female sex has always been how to account for it, given the supposed sexual enlightenment of the earlier works, particularly of the *Decameron*. The recent debate over the *Corbaccio*, reflecting this concern, lodges in the question of the date of its composition. While I shall sharply disagree with Giorgio Padoan, who has singlehandedly succeeded in opening the question concerning the dating of the work, I want to begin by admitting the logical necessity of his position. Almost all who had written about the *Corbaccio* took the work seriously and as the product of a radical change in Boccaccio's view of his literary vocation. That being the case, someone should have long ago fallen victim to the temptation to argue that the work was written much later than the *Decameron*. Since I do not find the standard view of the work the correct one, I have little by way of an interested point of view in this aspect of the debate; in my opinion, Boccaccio's purposes are far more constant than many suppose, as difficult as they may be to fathom. On the other hand, Padoan's attempted revision of the date of composition has had such an impact, and is so likely to continue to make it difficult to argue for a change in our sense of Boccaccio's intentions for the *Corbaccio*, that it seems necessary to discuss it at some length.

The history of discussion concerning the date of composition of the *Corbaccio* had been clearly set forth by Padoan.[58] Several aspects of his work will detain us: his finding that the *Corbaccio* was written in 1365 or 1366; his attempt to supply a textual justification for that finding; his apparent reasons for welcoming this solution; his other positive evidence for the later date.

Between 1742 (beginning with Manni's "discovery") and 1963, almost everyone who dealt with the text believed that §179 served to establish the age of the author at the time he composed the piece, 1354–55:

> E cominciando da quello che promesso abbiamo, dico che assai cagioni giustamente me e ogni altro possono muovere a doverti riprendere; ma acciò che tutte non si vadano ricercando, per fare il ragionamento minore, due solamente m'agrada toccarne: l'una è la tua età, la seconda sono gli tuoi studi; delle quali ciascuna per sé e amendune insieme ti doveano render cauto e guardingo dagli amorosi lacciuoli; e primieramente la tua età, la quale se le tempie già bianche e la canuta barba non m'ingannano, tu dovresti avere li costumi del mondo, fuori delle fasce già sono degli anni quaranta, e già son venticinque cominciatoli a conoscere.

> [Starting with that which we have promised, I declare that many reasons may justly cause me and anyone else to reproach you: but so as not to seek out all the causes, I would like to touch on only two of them to shorten the discussion: the first is your age: the second is your studies. Each of them in itself, and both together, should have made you cautious and circumspect about the traps of love. And first your age: if your temples already white and your grizzled beard do not deceive me, you, now some forty years out of swaddling clothes, should know the ways of the world—it is now twenty-five years since you began to learn them.]

We must certainly agree with Padoan, heeding Billanovich's early warning (1947:162–63), that any positive dating of the work on the basis of this passage is impossible.[59] At least it is Padoan's current view that such is the case. In 1963, however, he thought he could demonstrate that the passage referred to 1365 or 1366 as the year in which Boccaccio wrote the *Corbaccio*.

I do not mean to tax my friend's patience by returning to his earlier hypothesis, which now seems totally discredited. And I do not do so with any unpleasant motive. His error is one from which there is much to learn, and should be examined in order to clarify the nature of the problem which we face in trying to get a hold on this difficult little work. Padoan's intuition told him there was something wrong with the traditional text; he wrote to Nurmela and had his suspicion confirmed by the man who was editing the codices of the *Corbaccio*. To make a long story short, Padoan (1963:6), abetted by confirmation contained in a letter from Nurmela, adds the preposition "per" before "la quale," adjusts the punctuation of the passage, and has it refer not to the age of the narrator, but to that of the century, which is forty *plus* twenty-five, or sixty-five years old, thus making the date of the work 1365 or 1366. His words decribing the old hypothesis for a date of 1354–55 are strong: "l'interpretazione tradizionale appare assurda . . . davvero troppo sottile e fantasiosa" [the traditional interpretation seems absurd . . . indeed over-subtle and capricious] (1963:7).[60] However, and as Marti (1976:65n.) relates, Nurmela's edition (1968:19n.) revealed that the information which he had supplied to Padoan, based on an incomplete review of the codices, had been incorrect. There was in fact *no* codex which bore this reading. Thus, the only textual evidence which supported Padoan's new thesis had suddenly disappeared.

Now that Padoan's major evidence for his earlier hypothesis, evidence which he himself, following Marti's intervention (1976: 63–69), has abjured, may safely be discarded, we find instead Marti's revisionary argument. The author dates the time of his experience as 1354–55, while because of the likelihood that the text was written during Boccaccio's retreat to Certaldo (which Marti dates as 1363–66), we must deduce that the time of writing is later, if possibly a year or two earlier than Padoan had proposed. While Padoan has had to give up a single argument for his redating—even if it was his central one in 1963—he still receives support from Marti for what he apparently most wants: a "naturalist" Boccaccio from the beginnings through the *Decameron* and a "repentant" ("converted"?) Boccaccio after 1362.[61] Padoan's entire argument may be understood as depending on a central assumption, namely that Boccaccio *couldn't* have written such a text as a companion to the *Decameron*, as Padoan almost admits (1978:210):

> Il *Corbaccio* è ideologicamente e culturalmente assai lontano dal *Decameròn*, e non pare perciò probabile che esso sia stato composto immediatamente dopo il capolavoro, anche ammettendo che abbia agito il modello retorico del "remedium Amoris," di Ovidio e di Andrea Capellano.
>
> [The *Corbaccio* is ideologically and culturally quite distant from the *Decameron*, and it thus does not seem likely that it could have been composed immediately after the masterpiece, even if we admit that the rhetorical model of the *remedium Amoris*, of Ovid and Andreas Capellanus, had been operant.]

Boccaccio's Last Fiction

We shall return to Padoan's other evidence for a later date shortly. Now might it not be helpful to ask the question which precedes such an answer in another way? If the *Corbaccio* is in fact the compositional neighbor of the *Decameron*, whenever it was written, is it not probable that it reveals similar attitudes on the part of its creator (if not necessarily of its narrators)? I would argue that both views, the one offering us a womanizing Boccaccio in the *Decameron* or the one purveying a misogynist in the *Corbaccio*, are equally created by inauthentic readings, that Boccaccio's purpose was never to praise nor to blame the female sex, but to explore the effects of our sexual identities and desires upon women and men alike. I take this as the predominant concern of both these texts.

As I have attempted to demonstrate briefly in a finding which I hope will be buttressed by a forthcoming study,[62] important aspects of the stance of the author of the *Decameron* itself descend from that taken by the Ovid of the *Remedia amoris*. I hope to show that such is also the case for the *Corbaccio*, if not in the way that has been generally supposed. Perhaps more importantly, the texts which have most in common with the *Corbaccio* are indeed found in the *Decameron* and not elsewhere. No two *proemi* are as similar in all Boccaccio's corpus, as I have elsewhere made efforts to demonstrate;[63] *the* literary model for the narrative is found in *Decameron* VIII, 7. Thus models for both the stance of the author and for the essential narrative materials of the text are to be found in the *cento novelle* more readily than elsewhere.[64] And while one should always wish to err on the side of caution in dealing with Boccaccio's fictions as hidden autobiographies, following the pioneering work of Billanovich and Branca at mid-century, my guess is that Boccaccio is here dating his work, as he had previously "dated" the *Decameron* at IV, Introduction, 6, where he allows us to see him as verging on his forties:

> Altri, più maturamente mostrando di voler dire, hanno detto che alla mia età non sta bene l'andare omai dietro a queste cose, cioè a ragionar di donne o a compiacer loro.
>
> [Others, showing themselves desirous of more mature utterance, have said that, at my age, to pursue such activities as speaking of women or of attempting to give them pleasure is not fitting.]

Branca's note to this passage may seem to some too positivistic in its autobiographical focus: "'dalla mia prima giovanezza infino a questo tempo' aveva scritto il Boccaccio nel Proemio [3]: cioè sulla quarantina" ["from my earliest youth until now," Boccaccio had written in the Proemio (3): that is, as he was about to turn forty].[65] Nonetheless, it would seem reasonable to assume that Boccaccio knew that his readers would draw exactly such a biographical deduction from the passage. And, since, using Branca's research, we know that Boccaccio composed the work at almost exactly this age, it does fall out that the fictive narrator of the *Decameron* and its actual author do, in this and in other particulars, share elements of similar autobiographies (as is also the case, as has been frequently noted, in the *Corbaccio*), if not necessarily the same attitudes. Boccaccio obviously enjoyed such games. Within the fictional autobiographical incident which is the *Corbaccio*, all we should insist upon is that Boccaccio expects us to deal positivistically with the temporal clues offered by the passage at §179.[66] Thus, Boccaccio wanted to date the "events" (if not necessarily the writing) of the work as having occurred circa 1354. We may be able to draw no positive conclusion as to the date of composition from such evidence. On the other hand, we should rule out, just as certainly, the suppositious grounds put forward by Padoan and by Marti for the later dating.

In his second treatment of the dating of the *Corbaccio*, Padoan's other arguments for a later dating have remained intact. His 1978 article (to which the page numbers in parentheses in the following discussion refer) has only removed all argument based on the proposed textual variant. And I think it is fair to say that all his evidence presupposes a "serious" *Corbaccio*, a work at odds with all Boccaccio's previous work in fiction. Here, in brief, are Padoan's major pieces of evidence: The *Corbaccio* contains religious expressions only found in later work, especially the *Esposizioni* (212–15). The cult of the Virgin is reflected both in the *Corbaccio* and in the second draft of the *Genealogia*, especially the proem of Book IX, suggesting that for several years Boccaccio was willing to display publicly his personal devotion to Mary, but drew back from doing so in face of the stiffening Dominican hostility to such devotion, which became more firm in the 1350s (215–18).[67] In the *Decameron*, the Muses are seen as *donne*, while in the *Corbaccio*, they are seen as hostile to them (218–19). Dante is treated approvingly as a lover of women in the *Decameron* (IV, Intro., 33–34), but not in the first draft of the *Trattatello* (1351?–55)—an argument that does little for either side in the debate (220–21). All of these arguments presuppose that the author of the

Corbaccio is serious in his purpose. If he was playing with conventional misogynist literary traditions, the confrontations adduced by Padoan are valueless. And in all cases, it is clear, Padoan assumes a perfect identity between Boccaccio and his narrator. Thus, in my opinion, he is taking as axiomatic precisely the matter which is—or should be—in dispute.

A second set of evidentiary materials is then put forward, these based on supposed references to contemporary events: There is no reference in the *Corbaccio* to the political discord in Florence, which we find in the *Consolatoria a Pino de' Rossi* (1361), and Boccaccio was happy with the internal situation when he returned to the city in 1365. This argument is problematic for two reasons: first, there *is* reference to the troubles in the city (§300);[68] second, Padoan's thesis is now forced to envision the completion of the work in Florence in happier times (221), late 1365 or 1366, and is thus denied the comfort of at least some of Marti's support, which includes arguments for a slightly earlier dating. References to the Acciaiuoli family and to Queen Giovanna of Naples argue for the later dating (222–23).[69] Mention of Boccaccio's personal knowledge of solitude (§282) and the slighting reference to his weeding his onions (§459) both point to his stay in Certaldo (neither of which points lends any weight to the argument, since neither may logically be said to presuppose a return to Certaldo for Boccaccio to become acquainted with loneliness or to be aware of the chief agricultural product of his home town).

The last and lengthiest discussion considers why Boccaccio should have wanted to create a fictional date of 1354–55 in a work written in 1365–66. Padoan's first answer is that, as a cleric (ordained in 1360), Boccaccio now wants to place his sin into a more distant past so as not to disturb those who know him in his new role—to which one immediately replies that if this were a concern, he would not have written, or at least not published, the *Corbaccio* at all. Padoan's second answer concerns the love affair revealed in *Decameron* VIII, 7, with its sudden switch from youthful to aged scholar (which we have examined). According to Padoan, this is evidently an autobiographical reminiscence of Boccaccio's, one that reveals the fact that he has already had this troublesome affair by the time he was forty. This is a possible reading, of course, but one utterly devoid of even potential grounds of proof. All of these pieces of evidence were offered by Padoan in 1963 and then again, with minor refurbishing, in 1978. I think it is instructive that Marti, who agrees with Padoan's basic hypothesis, does not refer to even one of them to support his arguments for a later date.

Finally, we should glance at Padoan's only new piece of evidence offered in his reworking of the earlier article. He suggests (1978: 206) that Boccaccio himself (and for Padoan, like so many others, it is always a question of Boccaccio, never one of a narrator whose attitudes may be distinguishable from Boccaccio's) puts temporal distance between himself and his *innamoramento*, between "l'azione narrata e il momento della narrazione" [the action narrated and the moment of its telling], citing §6, a passage which serves my argument better than his. The passage runs as follows: "Non è ancora molto tempo passato che ... m'avenne che io fortissimamente sopra gli accidenti del carnale amore cominciai a pensare" [... not long ago ... I happened ... to begin thinking very hard about the vicissitudes of carnal love]. If we imagine that the text is being written in 1365 (or even 1366), how long ago is "not long ago"? A week? A month? Six months? A year? I don't know. But I do not think it means "twelve years ago." The passage serves far better to support the notion that the forty-one- or forty-two-year-old narrator is telling us some recent news, or, if we insist on Padoan's dating, that the fifty-two- or fifty-three-year-old narrator is referring to events which occurred well after 1355.

As I have suggested, all of Padoan's arguments seem to me to be predicated on a central predisposition, one that would have us believe that the *Corbaccio* has to be a late work because it is so different from all the fictions which precede it. Padoan, for instance, speaks of "quell'adesione entusiasta al mito cortese della «servitù d'amore»" [that enthusiastic adhesion to the courtly myth of "love service"] which extends from the early works through the *Decameron* and which he finds absent from the *Corbaccio*.[70] He thus offers as evidence exactly what should be seen as a matter of dispute, namely, whether or not the *Corbaccio* is to be read as a straightforward confession. There are those of us, not many as yet, perhaps, who will argue that to take the *Corbaccio* at its face value is to fail to deal with its author's playful and ironic manipulation of his materials.[71] Dating his text in this way allows him to wink at his friends, who know whatever "facts" to which he may allude. For purposes of his fiction these facts may or may not include a widow who spurned him (given the widow of *Decameron* VIII, 7, I would guess that there was no such incident, that it is a literary event alone)—we will never know unless better documentation falls into our hands. But I would also guess that the allusion to forty-one or forty-two years of life does in fact refer, at least approximately, to Boccaccio's age when he was composing the *Corbaccio*, as does the reference to his nearing his *quarantina* at the time of the writing of the *Decameron*, the "action" of which transpired some years earlier (1348), when he was thirty-five.

Given Branca's succinct and convincing treatment, we now universally accept a date for the composition of the earlier work as 1351–53; I own myself morally convinced, as the French say, that the *Corbaccio* was in fact composed soon after the completion of the masterpiece. However, all that one can say with certainty is that Boccaccio embedded texts in the two works which *ask* his reader to consider him as being nearly forty as he was one-third of the way through composing the first one, and barely forty-two as he wrote the second. Whether this was in fact the case we cannot know. But we should be far more open to the patent gesture made by the maneuver, which is to tell us, as straightforwardly as Boccaccio will ever do, that *Decameron* and *Corbaccio* are meant to be read as closely contiguous literary experiences, whether they were so or not. These two texts tell us more about one another than we may learn from most other sources about the essential strategies of either. And their mutual relation to the essential strategies of the amatory texts of Ovid is one of the most important and least explored aspects of both works. We will turn next to a brief consideration of the problems caused by the title of the work, a discussion that will not be without Ovidian concerns, before examining some perhaps more important relations between these two writers.

THE MEANING OF THE TITLE

I shall not attempt a review of the many suggestions regarding the possible sources and meanings of the title of the *Corbaccio*.[72] Most contemporary students of the problem agree, at least generally, that the primary field of meaning of the title is avian (*corbo* ← *corvo*) and disparaging (*-accio*). And most also agree that the essential reference of the title is to the widow.[73] In my brief earlier discussion of the problem (1977: 139–40), I suggested several points which I still consider worth pursuing. First, I argued that, while the title assuredly is meant to refer to the widow, it was also meant to indicate the work itself.[74] I still maintain that this is very probably the case. Not only is the widow a *corbaccia*, but the book itself is ugly and crow-like.[75] I would add that if the *Decameron* is a "Galeotto," as its subtitle indicates, a go-between to join men to women (whatever the eventual intent of the self-description), this book is a "contra-Galeotto," meant to keep men and women apart (whatever the eventual intent of *that* self-description). The title then, is meant to refer both to widow and to book.

I also suggested, tentatively indeed, that the nine letters of the title only fail by a single letter to constitute an anagram of Boccaccio's name, that is, "Corbaccio" implies "Borcaccio." To my delight, I now find that Paul Watson has allowed himself to consider this possibility—if he too is tentative: "In this connection Hollander . . . observes that Boccaccio's story does have its references to Boccaccio's own life as a man of letters, without becoming an autobiography, and that his title here plays with the letters of his own name; in that vein 'Boccaccio' can also be translated 'big mouth'."[76]

My only disappointment with Professor Watson is that he, like everyone else, as far as I can tell, has not chosen to deal with the third element in my earlier discussion. It is one which I continue to believe is of considerable importance. I suggested that Boccaccio's choice of a title closely reflected that of Ovid's *Ibis*, a similarly avian-titled satirical attack upon an avian-named enemy, a work which Boccaccio copied in his own hand.[77] I should like to take a moment to remind or advise the reader of the content of Ovid's biting satire.[78] The work begins with fifty-year-old Ovid (1) in exile in Pontus, claiming that he has never before intentionally harmed anyone with his poetry ("Omne fuit Musae carmen inerme meae"—2). Yet now he wishes to take merciless revenge on an unnamed enemy who, back in Rome, seeks further offense to Ovid's already ruined life and reputation (11–14).[79] The piece is modeled on a satire by Callimachus (who is mentioned, under the name of Battiades, at verse 55, along with his satiric attack upon Ibis) and is primarily given over to a lengthy (644 verses) elegiac (see vv. 45–46) explosion against this enemy.[80] The bulk of the text is replete with a string of horrible deaths recalled from the ample storehouse of Greek and Latin antiquity, any and all of which are wished upon the nameless intended victim, who may be known for the time being, says Ovid, as "Ibis" ("Ibidis interea tu quoque nomen habe"—62). Ovid's poisonous wish for his enemy runs as follows (vv. 63–64): "Utque mei versus aliquantum noctis habebunt, / Sic vitae series tota sit atra tuae" [And as my verses have something of darkness about them, thus may the sequence of all your days be black]. At the conclusion of this "little book," Ovid issues a final curse in his envoy: "Ibis" may herewith receive notice that his exiled enemy has not forgotten him; as brief as is his text, he hopes the gods will send even more woe upon his foe than he has sought himself and thus multiply his darkest hopes.[81] The final two verses may well remind us of passages near and at the conclusion of the *Corbaccio*: "*Postmodo plura leges* et nomen habentia verum, / *Et pede quo debent acria bella geri*" (italics added) [soon enough will you read still more {such curses}, now bearing your own true name, and {written} in the meter in which still fiercer warfare should be carried on].

Boccaccio's narrator also hints at a second attack on his victim in another form (his will be in verse rather than in prose, while Ovid will change his elegiacs for iambics): "... senza che io m'ingegnerò con più perpetuo verso testimonianza delle sue malvage e disoneste opere lasciare a' futuri" [unless, that is, I exert myself to leave to future generations witness of her wicked and indecent acts in the more lasting form of verse] (535). He hopes that his literary violence will be followed by God's still harsher punishment (Ovid's greater pain will be more and greater literary harm, while the Boccaccian narrator wants still sterner, realer stuff): "ed ella è da pugnere con più aguto stimolo che tu non porti teco" [she is to be stung by a sharper goad than you bear with you] (561).

The two vengeful texts, *Ibis* and *Corbaccio*, seem to be related, not only in such particulars as these, but in their genre, authorial stance, and apparent intent. And this relation is one, if we grant its existence, which would cast an interesting light on the literary nature of Boccaccio's management of his last fiction.

OVID AND THE STRATEGIES OF REMEDYING LOVE

Whether or not the preceding argument has convinced the reader that Boccaccio had the *Ibis* in mind as he composed the *Corbaccio*, it seems indisputably clear that the *Remedia amoris* is as close as we can come to finding the essential classical model for the work.[82] And while this statement is not likely to find much opposition, it is also true that it has less company than one might expect. Many, in our time, acknowledge the general appositeness of the *Remedia*,[83] but few have discussed the relationship between the two works with more than general remarks or passing notice. And yet it seems fairly clear that Boccaccio's essential stance as writer depends more upon his sense of Ovid's purposes in the *Remedia* than on any other classical precursor's.[84]

If the *Decameron* begins where the *Remedia amoris* ends, the *Corbaccio* begins with a glancing reference to its beginning.[85] Our narrator, at the early stages of his self-revelation as unhappy lover, comes to the crucial moment of the result of his amatory misadventure, that of his inner debate as to whether or not he should do away with himself (10–12). At this point, the method of his projected suicide is not mentioned. It is only later that the guide will make this plain to us, first when he imagines the suicidal act that would please the lover's hardhearted mistress as "lo 'mpiccarti per la gola" [hanging yourself by the throat] (34), and then again, near the conclusion: "ti saresti per la gola impiccato" [you would have hanged yourself by the neck] (468). This method of revealing the means of self-destruction envisioned by the narrator calls attention to the detail. And while it has an explanation in Boccaccio's awareness of the commonality of hanging as a particularly Florentine form of suicide,[86] there is also reason to believe that Boccaccio intended that his words echo a passage in the *Remedia* (15–18):[87]

> At siquis male fert indignae regna puellae,
>   Ne pereat, nostrae sentiat artis opem.
> Cur aliquis laqueo collum nodatus amator
>   A trabe sublimi triste pependit onus?
>
> [Yet if anyone unjustly bears the rule of an unworthy mistress, lest he perish, let him hear the helpfulness of my skill. Why has a lover knotted the noose about his neck and hung, mournful weight, from a lofty beam?]

Boccaccio's *Corbaccio*, like Ovid's *Remedia amoris*, is a witty work apparently aimed at saving suicidal disappointed lovers from their intended fates. In both cases, such concerns serve more as pretexts than as genuine concerns.

As we know, most medieval readers of the *Remedia* took the work as a serious attack upon love by a reformed lover.[88] As is apparent from all the previous treatments which have suggested that there is a significant relation between the *Remedia* and the *Corbaccio*, such is the way in which its

Boccaccio's Last Fiction

relevance to Boccaccio's text has been conceived.[89] However, when we consider that Boccaccio himself was fully aware that the *Remedia* was a companion piece to the *Ars*, composed early in Ovid's career,[90] we might begin to suspect that he was a more sensitive reader of Ovid's concluding amatory work than he is generally taken to be. The *Remedia amoris* does not in fact offer serious *remedium* at all. It is a far better view to understand that the *Ars* (as well as the *Amores*) is a work which mocks lovers for their ridiculous behaviors. By showing us what lovers do, it surely expects us rather to recognize their folly than willfully to imitate them. It is a dull reader indeed who comes from a reading of these works believing he or she has heard the voice of a celebrant sensualist. We can only imagine how Naso felt, when he found himself treated as such, or at any rate treated as having written of scabrous things and thus immorally. He surely seems, like the Boccaccian narrator of the *Decameron* in this instance, to have felt cornered by his critics, whether these were real or imagined. The *Remedia* was his rejoinder. We might remind ourselves of its essential contents and strategies.

To Cupid, angered by the name and title of this *libellus* (1–2),[91] Ovid responds that he is not backsliding, that he is still a lover (3–12). Let those who love happily continue on; his only purpose is to aid those lovers who undergo the threat of imminent death under the harsh rule of an unworthy woman (13–16). He begs Cupid to help such as these, bringing them either happy love or, if unhappy, at least freedom from suicidal impulse (17–38). Under these conditions, Cupid, with a shake of his jewelled wings, encourages him to complete his task (39–40). The proem of the *Remedia*, even read "straight," thus promises nothing of the total war against Love that the young god putatively feared to find or that many of Ovid's readers have in fact found in it. Playful Ovid is reminding us that what he has apparently praised in his last work, libidinous behavior, is either as culpable or as blameless as it was then. The reader's view of it depends entirely on his or her own desires. A perception of the ludicrous, self-centered, and antisocial behavior of Ovidian lovers is all that we should require to understand that the author of *Amores* and *Ars amatoria* is first of all an ironist. The opening of the *Remedia*, pledging continued loyalty to Cupid, should put us on warning. What follows surely does, or at least ought to.

The *pars executiva* of the *Remedia* falls into two large sections. The first

(41–356), addressed to disappointed lovers, men *and* women (41, 49), teaches how to avoid dependence on those who do not love them in return. The second (397–814) shows us how to learn to control our sexual appetites, even as we indulge them, so as to avoid being conquered by love while we enjoy its fruit. It, too, has a proemium of forty verses (357–396), in which the poet, seeking our indulgence for the frankness of his following discourse, complains about certain of his readers (361–362): "Nuper enim nostros quidam carpsere libellos, / Quorum censura Musa proterva mea est" [For recently some, in whose censure my Muse is held to be shameless, have complained of my little books]. His words may well remind us of the similar defense raised against one set of Boccaccio's (imagined?) detractors in the *Decameron*, those who hold or will hold against him his licentious bearing as writer.[92]

The rest of this interruption of the docent role, which he affects for the bulk of the *Remedia*, is concerned with his stance as poet (365–396). Attributing the hostility of his detractors to envy—a charge Boccaccio also will make[93]—Ovid contrives to make himself the new Homer (to their Zoilus), his elegiac meter the equal of Homeric hexameter, his comedy as lofty as the subject of the tragedians. The negative *tertium quid* for both himself and Homer is satire. Callimachus's iambics do not suit either poet: noble hexameter Homer and love-singing elegiac Ovid are presented as the true poets, not Callimachus.[94] Leaving Achilles to Homeric utterance, but preserving Cydippe for his own, he goes on to contrast Homeric Andromache to Ovidian Thais. She is named four times in as many lines (383–386)—the densest repetition of any name in all of Ovid's work, I believe, with the concluding and triumphant phrase, "Thais in arte mea est" [in my art Thais lives], occurring twice for emphasis. Homer sings heroes, Ovid sings whores. It is a daring and wonderful moment and is crowned with the assertive comparison which Ovid, from the beginning, has evidently been most desirous of making: Elegy owes as much to him as epic does to Virgil.[95] The passage may have found its way to the *Corbaccio* when the guide urges his charge to associate with the Muses and not with widows: "e teco, poiché i versi d'Omero, di Virgilio e degli altri antichi valorosi avranno cantati, i tuoi medesimi, se tu vorrai, canteranno" [after they have sung with you the verses of Homer, Virgil, and other worthy ancients, they will sing your own, if you wish] (285). If this is a reminiscence of Ovid's wonderful passage, its equivalence of Homer, Virgil, and the *remedium*-minded narrator is even less believable than the one offered by Ovid on his own behalf, a Boccaccian joke piled upon an Ovidian wink.

Like the *Remedia*, the *Decameron* is structured on three authorial interventions: one at its beginning, one before its middle, one at its conclusion. And like the *Remedia*, the *Corbaccio* gives its author's blue-nosed detractors what they apparently most crave: an attack on women, who are no more than whores. After the *Remedia* Ovid wrote no more *libelli* about women; after the *Corbaccio* Boccaccio left vernacular fiction behind him—at least "officially"—to pursue more Petrarchan pursuits. I will return to this point in my concluding remarks. What I think is most important about the *Remedia* is its playfulness. It is in fact little more than a continuation of the *Ars*, its fourth part, masquerading as an attack on the earlier work. And I would hope that the reader would want to add that the *Corbaccio* shares a similar relationship with the *Decameron*.

If the *Remedia* is Boccaccio's model classical text for the *Corbaccio* (although the sixth *Satire* of Juvenal is clearly its most visited classical source), why does the work contain so few evident quotations of Ovid's *libellus*? My answer to that question is in two parts. First, the voices which we hear for the most part in the *Corbaccio* are those of embittered misogynists, "Juvenals," as it were, while the urbane and balanced Ovid of the *Remedia* is primarily present outside the work, manipulating it and us. Thus, we do not so much hear his voice as sense his authorial stance and strategy. Second, Boccaccio had presented himself as the Ovid of the *Remedia* in the *Decameron*'s authorial frames, especially the *Proemio*.[96] There, that presence may have seemed surprising. Here, it seems normal (and many have sensed its appropriateness as model), so much so that it does not require textual citations to signal its applicability. And thus, if the *Decameron* is, in its profoundly playful way, first presented as a *remedium*, it is perhaps inevitable that the *Corbaccio*, only apparently attacking the values of the *Decameron*, should be perceived as an apparent *remedium remedii amoris*, while in fact being a work which continues the strategies of its precursor rather than undermining them.

THE PRESENCE OF DANTE IN THE *CORBACCIO*

The extensive presence of the texts of Dante in the *Corbaccio* has not received widespread attention. Until recently, there has been little work of interest, indeed little work at all, which is concertedly and frontally directed to this aspect of any of Boccaccio's works. Carlo Delcorno's important study of the *Elegia di madonna Fiammetta* is a major exception.[97] It now seems clearer than it did even several years ago that no literary source—perhaps not all the other literary sources put together—had as great or as consistent an effect on Boccaccio as the works of Dante. Appendix 1 of this study is presented in the hope that its findings, unadorned by commentary, will suggest how extensively Dante's texts have penetrated the *Corbaccio*. Some of these citations have naturally enough found their way into my remarks about particular passages in that text. From these, my general sense of the parodic use to which they are being put in Boccaccio's satire is evident.

This parody, it seems to me, cuts two ways. First, it trivializes the seriousness with which the narrator presents himself. I choose an example with which I have not yet dealt: ". . . che se col vero corpo la montagna salita avessi che nel sogno mi parve salire" [as if I had climbed with my real body the mountain which it seemed to me I had climbed in my dream] (555). This is the response of the narrator upon awakening from his dream. It is obviously meant to be taken as a reflection of the similar concern expressed in *Paradiso* I, 73–75:

> S'i' era sol di me quel che creasti
> novellamente, amor che 'l ciel governi,
> tu 'l sai, che col tuo lume mi levasti.
>
> [Whether I was only that part of me which You created last, Love who governs heaven, You know, Who raised me up with Your light.]

Dante's solemn Pauline wonderment as to whether or not he was in heaven in soul alone or in body also has an amusing counterpart in the narrator's less dramatic version of a similar question: Was his body in the company of his soul during his dream?[98] This is not amusing, or particularly worth noting, unless we know our Dante and perceive the interplay of the two texts. A passage which we might otherwise read straight through without pausing for thought suddenly stands out from the page when we see it for what it is. But if it serves to make the narrator look foolish, a would-be Dante made of humbler stuff indeed, it also has a reverse effect. The *Commedia*'s claims for direct experience of God's heaven, because of this juxtaposition, are called into question. I think that whenever Boccaccio resorts to this aspect of Dante's poem (especially when Dante's otherworldly experiences are coupled with claims for utter truthfulness), he tends to be playful, acknowledging the force of Dante's claims but also making clear his own dubiety about them. He knows, he contrives to let us perceive, that Dante's vision, too, is a *favola*. Thus, the pull between high and low mimetic modes goes in both directions. The Boccaccian "climber" falls flat on his face, but even as he falls, he pulls the great vision back with him toward earth.

An inevitable result of these many transactions between Boccaccio's texts and Dante's, once we see them, is our recognition of how assured Boccaccio was that his art was capable of standing next to Dante's without embarrassment. We may not all agree that the *Amorosa Visione* is a worthy imitation of the *Commedia* (if Boccaccio obviously thought that it was), but I have heard no complaints about the artistic worth of the *Decameron*, a work that we are only beginning to see as constant reproducer of Dantean text.

As is evident from a consultation of Appendix 1, many of Boccaccio's citations of Dante are merely that, a tessera picked out of one mosaic and inserted into another with little apparent concern for what the other pattern might have suggested about the new work. Boccaccio obviously treated Dante's texts with a respect hitherto reserved in early modern Europe only for the works of Latin antiquity. And he equally obviously knew Dante's language so well that he sometimes forgot that he was speaking it. Insofar as this is true, it makes a critic's task difficult, at best. When do we confront a "crucial" borrowing, bringing with it a sure sense of the context of the original? When a "significant" citation which throws light on the present text by reminding us, at least in large contours, of a moment in the precursor's? When a "glancing" reference? When an "unconscious" regurgitation? We have no sure, firm rules to govern such exercises of our judgment, we must rely solely on memory and intuition, exercising reasonable caution and awaiting the opinions of our peers.[99] These difficulties do not urge us to give over such enterprises; they do urge us to undertake them with care. I would add that while I think some of the citations found in my appendix are clearly seen, others are less certain, and still other conjunctions may not really have been on Boccaccio's mind at all. Yet I wonder how many other clear echoes my predecessors and I have simply failed to hear.[100]

Perhaps nothing is as important about the frequent presence of Dante in the *Corbaccio* as the fact itself. If we may not all agree on the shadings of meaning or consequences for interpretation conferred by these citations, one thing is clear and certain. A work that is so deeply involved in the intricacies of another is more than merely unlikely to have been written by a jilted old man, bent solely on revenge. Dante's presence in the *Corbaccio*, on the average more than once per page, reveals that the *Corbaccio* is a text written by a writer who was fully in possession of himself and of his artistic patrimony as clearly as does the careful structuring of the work, with which subject we began this investigation.

In this study I have argued, not for the first time—to Barricelli (1975) belongs that honor—that the *Corbaccio* is not a "serious" satire, but one which turns back on itself, revealing its misogynous major characters to be male hysterics, latter-day haters of womankind because of their own weaknesses and failings. If I am right, and if others are convinced that I am, then we will have entered a third stage of critical attitudes toward the work. The first, from Manni (1742) up to Billanovich (1947), took the text to be autobiographical and misogynous; the second, from Billanovich to Barricelli (1975), asserted that the work was not autobiography but fiction, while it continued to take its misogyny seriously. Barricelli may have ushered in the "new age" in criticism of the *Corbaccio*, an age in which the work is held to be an ironic fiction, if no one has listened to him, not even the younger present writer.[101]

If that is the better view, why has it been so difficult to achieve? (I am aware that many of my readers will be far from granting that it *is* the better view.) The very fact that this is Boccaccio's last fiction, one which seems to constitute the traditional concluding retraction which we expect of medieval writers who deal with secular subjects from a secular point of view, makes it seem more likely to be serious than playful. And yet such a view also requires that we dismiss the *Corbaccio* as the work of a writer who has lost his touch. Whatever else the present study has accomplished, I hope that it has demonstrated that Boccaccio was still the master of his craft when he composed his last fiction. How, then, can we explain Boccaccio's motives for writing his "anti-" *Vita Nuova, La Vita Vecchia*, as it were? In conclusion, I would like to offer my own sense of the most likely hypothesis.

If Boccaccio wrote the *Decameron* as a work which was less interested in praising or blaming human behavior than in exploring it, and if he presented the work, in his *Proemio*, as being closely related to Ovid's *Remedia amoris*, his own remarks about his audiences in the introduction to *Decameron* IV and at the work's conclusion may give us some sense of what sort of response he either anticipated or perhaps actually received. If both those who praised and blamed him missed his point, took him to be making either an unwarranted attack on normative morality or to be championing actual mores, if, in short, his carefully wrought *capolavoro* was presented to blind eyes, how might he have responded? If I were Boccaccio and found myself in that situation, I might very well have attempted a *Corbaccio*. In our American vernacular, I would have "given them the bird." If his readers did not understand his ironic *Remedium*, by God he would give them a *Remedium* they could understand—or thought they could. The *Corbaccio* tells so tall a tale that Boccaccio believed that no one could possibly take it seriously. Given the fact that it took precisely six hundred years from the year of his death (1375) for someone finally to understand his basic plan, we must judge him to have been wildly optimistic about our abilities as readers. A man has to hope.

The *Corbaccio* was meant, I think, to give his detractors what they seemed to want. At the same time its author was mocking them by presenting an Ovidian monster, a *remedium* become a disease, hoping (like Ovid) that if his enemies would not fathom his purpose, then at least his friends might. In my interpretation of the *Corbaccio* I find Boccaccio poor in friends indeed. And I think he may have felt a sense of isolation, of having labored for those unworthy of his talent. If he did so, that feeling may explain at least as well as any other hypothesis why it was that the *Corbaccio* was the last fiction written by Giovanni Boccaccio. He now put all his energies into living the literary life recommended and exemplified by Petrarch, a life which cared little publicly for vernacular fiction (if enough to refurbish *Amorosa Visione* and *Decameron*—but those were already written) and devoted itself to humanist exercises, in Latin or in Italian (those which continue to champion the works of Dante), while not risking any more vernacular fiction. He had had enough of us because we simply were not up to him. Who can blame him for that?

Cadenabbia, Good Friday 1987

NOTES

1. The text of the *Corbaccio* to which I shall refer is Nurmela's (1968), which is also available as reproduced, with some changes, by Marti (1972). (We have still to look forward to the publication of Giorgio Padoan's new edition of the text in the Mondadori series of the *Opere*.) English translations of the *Corbaccio* are drawn from Cassell (1975); divergences from his renderings have been placed in curly brackets. The text of the *Decameron* which I have used is vol. 4 of *Tutte le opere di Giovanni Boccaccio*, ed. Vittore Branca (Milan: Mondadori, 1976); translations of passages from that work are my own. Other citations refer to works listed in my Bibliography, which is in part derived from that found in Cassell's translation (1975): 165–83. I have made no attempt to represent the totality of previous work (for such a listing see Cassell), only including those items which precede Cassell's translation when they are pertinent to my discussion or were absent from his bibliography. On the other hand, I have tried to refer to all publications concerned with the *Corbaccio* which issued after the appearance of Cassell's book, whether or not I refer to them.

The first research on this essay was performed for a faculty seminar which I offered at Dartmouth College during August of 1984. I wish particularly to remember the efforts of Professor Stephen G. Nichols, Jr., now at the University of Pennsylvania but then the Chairman of the Department of French & Italian at Dartmouth, in creating the opportunity for the seminar to take place, but I also take the liberty of hoping that my colleagues in that seminar, including Professor Nichols, will find this study a memento of some time spent pleasantly and instructively in good company and in a pleasant place, as I do. My final draft was composed in April of 1987 at the *foresteria* of the Villa Ronconi, that beautiful place above Lake Como given to Princeton University for the *otium* of its professors by Avv. Pompeo Maresi. It is difficult to think of more congenial surroundings in which to think of Boccaccio, Dante, and Ovid—or of anything else. I wish to express my gratitude to Margherita Frankel, Frank Ordiway, Lauren Scancarelli Seem, and an anonymous reader, all of whom made numerous helpful suggestions. And I must offer my thanks yet again to the Princeton University Committee for Research in the Humanities and the Social Sciences for helping to defray the costs of publication.

2. More recently we have the similar judgment of Per Nykrog (1984), who considers the *Corbaccio* to be "a joke, a parody—not of Dante: of sinister and embittered misogyny" (439). Angela M. Iovino (1983) also strongly opposes the traditional interpretation of the text. She does not go as far as Barricelli and Nykrog

45

Notes

in perceiving the ironic and humorous nature of Boccaccio's last vernacular fiction; rather, she chooses to argue for a more serious and pro-female Boccaccio both in the *Decameron* and in the *Corbaccio*. In this connection, see also Marina Scordilis Brownlee, "Hermeneutics in the *Corbacho*," in *Medieval Texts and Contemporary Readers*, ed. Laurie A. Finke and Martin B. Schichtman (Ithaca, N.Y.: Cornell University Press, 1987), 216–33. Her discussion of Talavera's fifteenth-century work (which is treated by Nykrog in a similar spirit) argues that the misogyny of the *Corbacho* is rather to be considered playful—a witty reversal of the *De amore* of Andreas Capellanus—than serious.

3. For a similar understanding of a chiasmic arrangement of the first nine Days of the *Decameron* see Janet Smarr, "Symmetry and Balance in the *Decameron*," *Medievalia* 2 (1976), 159–87.

4. For a review of such readings see Barricelli (1975), 96–101.

5. See Appendix 2, "The Proem of the *Corbaccio:* Sources and Analogues," for an attempt to demonstrate connections among the Boccaccian narrator of the *Decameron*, Dante Alighieri, and the speaker to whom we attend here. See also my forthcoming study of the *Proemio* of the *Decameron* in the first volume of the *Lectura Boccaccii* sponsored by the American Boccaccio Association.

6. This passage is reminiscent of *Vita Nuova* XIV. Boccaccio's "battaglia" (12) reflects "la battaglia de li diversi pensieri" [the battle of opposing thoughts] (XIV, 1), which brings the protagonist of the *libello* to a moment of crisis. He confides in a friend and then returns to his room: "mi ritornai ne la camera de le lagrime; ne la quale, piangendo e vergognandomi, fra me stesso dicea . . ." [I returned to the chamber of my tears, in which, weeping and ashamed, I said to myself . . .] (XIV, 9). The scene in the *Corbaccio* seems to be built out of elements in this chapter in the *Vita Nuova:* ". . . ritrovandom'io solo nella mia camera, la quale è veramente sola testimonia della mie lagrime" [finding myself alone in my chamber (which truly is the only witness of my tears)] (6). Boccaccio's narrator bears a striking, if obverse, similarity to Dante's. His "amico" will be internalized as his *pensiero.*

7. See Benvenuto da Imola's appreciation of the negative tone of the interjection *deh* (as it appears in *Purgatorio* XI, 37): "dictio deprecativa est."

8. See Hollander, "The Sun Rises in Dante," *Studi sul Boccaccio* 14 (1983–84): 243n.–244n. My forthcoming study of the *Proemio*, undertaken under the auspices of the American Boccaccio Association, develops the connection. For a treatment of the *Proemio*, with which I share many points of agreement—especially its sense of the importance of the *Remedia amoris* to Boccaccio's strategies—see Kirkham (1985).

9. Here I should like to offer a retraction of my own strong statement on this point (Hollander, 1977), 142, n. 47, and my conjoined attack on Cassell's view (1974). I there took the *odium* of the narrator as justified, Aristotle's and Thomas's "just hatred of that which should be hated," while Cassell had argued, citing Boccaccio's own words (*Esposizioni sopra la Comedia di Dante*, ed. Giorgio Padoan; *Tutte le opere di Giovanni Boccaccio*, ed. Vittore Branca, vol. 6 [Milan: Mondadori, 1965]: *Inferno* VII, esp. all. 111), that the narrator displays "un disordinato appetito di vendetta." I am now convinced that Cassell is correct. Iovino (1983), 175–76 also embraces this view.

Notes

10. For my earlier opinion that complaints against Fortune, which appear frequently enough in Boccaccio's characters and narrators, are to be taken ironically and not as self-revealing complaint to be taken at face value, see Hollander (1977), 179, n. 106. It is my view that, from the very beginning of his career as writer, Boccaccio was always aware of the restraint imposed by Boethius's *Consolatio* upon such lamentation.

11. Indeed 54 of the approximately 125 citations of Dante in the *Corbaccio* which are offered below occur between §54 and §131. See Appendix 1.

12. For both citations, see Appendix 1, *ad loc.*

13. It is probably not a coincidence that our first view of the spirit-guide (66–67) reveals that he descends from a perhaps surprising Dantean model, the Cato of *Purgatorio* I: ". . . e ecco, . . . venir verso me con lento passo un uomo senza alcuna compagnia . . . di statura grande, di pelle e di pelo bruno, benché in parte bianco divenuto fosse per gli anni. . . ." [. . . behold, . . . a solitary man was slowly making his way toward me . . . of great stature . . . with dark skin and hair (though partly white {because of} his age) . . .]. See *Purgatorio* I, 30–36: "vidi presso di me un veglio solo, / degno di tanta reverenza in vista, / che più non dee a padre alcun figliuolo. / Lunga la barba e di pel bianca mista / portava, a' suoi capelli simigliante, / de' quai cadeva al petto doppia lista" [and near me I saw a solitary old man, worthy, by his appearance, of so great veneration that no son owes more to his father. The hair of his beard was long, with an admixture of white, like the hair on his head, whence a double tress fell upon his breast]. Boccaccio's account of Cato's dismissal of his wife, Marcia (*Esposizioni, Inferno* IV, esp. litt., 237) intrinsically presents Cato as willing cuckold. Cato, says Boccaccio, not wanting further carnal concourse with women, allowed her to go to another man, Hortensius, "imaginando non dovere per l'età essere a lei questa astinenzia possibile" [imagining that, because of her age, such abstinence would not be possible for her]. An old man offended by his younger wife's sexual appetite is a familiar appurtenance of Boccaccian fiction. And since so much else about the guide reminds us generically of the role played by Virgil in Dante's poem, Boccaccio's later sense that Marcia was still sexually active when she was sent away by Cato helps us to ascertain a further reason for his choice of Catonic iconography for the first appearance of the guide.

14. Thus the third and seventh sections of the work, balanced as they are, the first presenting Boccaccio's brief version of Dante's Hell, the second, Purgatory, are further related by their chiasmic inner structure: vision of Hell followed by dialogue, dialogue followed by vision of Purgatory.

15. We may think of Virgil in *Purgatorio* XIX, 34–35, who is perhaps there to be understood as calling on Dante by name. If there (as here) the name is suppressed, it will sound vibrantly enough on the lips of Beatrice in *Purgatorio* XXX, 55.

16. We should probably think again of Dante, who never names Florence in the course of the *Vita Nuova*. Boccaccio will refer to "i Fiorentini" (379) once in the course of the *Corbaccio*, just often enough to let us know that he has them in mind and to make us focus on the name of the city which is home to these characters. Marti (1976), 84 and n. comments upon the Florentine setting of the work.

Notes

17. For discussion of autobiography as literary creation, if referring not to Boccaccio but to some of his continental fourteenth-century contemporaries, see G. B. Gybbon-Monypenny, "Autobiography in the *Libro de buen amor* in the Light of Some Literary Comparisons," *Bulletin of Hispanic Studies* 34 (1957): 63–78; "Guillaume de Machaut's Erotic 'Autobiography': Precedents for the Form of the *Voir-Dit*," in *Studies in Medieval Literature and Languages in Memory of Frederick Whitehead*, ed. W. Rothwell et al. (Manchester: Manchester University Press, 1973), 133–52.

18. For the traditional misogynist sources of this section of the work, see Cassell (1975), xix–xxi and the notes in Nurmela's text. Cassell's notes frequently reflect Nurmela's, but at times add particulars not found in the preceding volume. The "authorities" most frequently cited include Juvenal (his sixth *Satire*), St. Jerome, Theophrastus, misogynist passages in the *Roman de la rose*, and a small assemblage of woman-despising clergy. To this list should be added the *De arte amandi* of Andreas Capellanus, which is also frequently alluded to, and in such a way as to make it a fellow-traveler in the crusade against women.

19. This passage, as do some others, includes imagined unpleasant discourse addressed by the woman to the man, the only interruptions allowed in an oratorical performance which consumes nearly one-fifth of the work.

20. The balanced chiasmic structure which is so often visible in the *Corbaccio* is also revealed by the ordering of material in this seemingly uncontrolled vituperation: particular, general; general, particular.

21. We may remember that the narrator's first awareness of the widow came through the words of praise offered by a friend of her departed husband's (135) and thus come to suspect that Boccaccio intended to portray such genteel panders in the worst possible light.

22. The refutation of her constancy mirrors the earlier general attack on female flightiness (245–246), where we are told that women are inconstant in all things but lust—exactly what we are now told about the rewidowed widow.

23. The word reappears here to indicate what unhappy lovers want to see visited upon their women. We heard it first in this sense from the *pensiero* at §45; it had been used twice by the guide himself to indicate both the absence of desire for revenge for small sins in God's justice (113) and the justness of the *vendetta* which He does exact in our penitence (118). Thus, both the "thought" and the guide conclude their persuasions with reference to the motivation which is—or will soon be—so evidently the narrator's own.

24. His behavior here, coupled with the many proofs which he himself offers of the men who desired his wife, may make us wonder how much we should trust his vituperative presentation of his wife's ugliness and shrewishness. In Iovino's words (1983, 172), "The *Corbaccio* is ironic and ridicules not the female sex but lovelorn men." I am less sure than she that women come off better than men in the work, and would prefer a formulation which sees all of us as equally tainted, or at least one which insisted that our sexual identities had nothing to do with our moral natures, which may be as good as we are molded (and mold ourselves) to be.

25. The guide insists upon the possibility of this new-found hatred being also the source of the eventual salvation of the widow in two other statements: §526, 529. These are the major gestures of kindness which he makes toward his former

Notes

wife and which conform to his state as penitent in Purgatory. As we will see, they will find no counterpart in the narrator's understanding of his ensuing mission.

26. Boccaccio's formulation of the epideictic aims of writers, with its insistence on the willfulness inherent in their decisions regarding who is praised and who is blamed (in this instance, who gets to heaven, who to hell), would hardly seem to mean to leave Dante unscathed. For a treatment of Boccaccio's involvement in the techniques of epideictic rhetoric, see Craig Kallendorf, "Boccaccio's Dido and Rhetorical Criticism of Virgil's *Aeneid*," *Studies in Philology* 82 (1985): 401–15.

27. Even a critic as aware of the playfulness of the *Corbaccio* as Cassell (1975, 149, in his note to this passage) takes this announcement of a putative choice between verse and prose as an indication that Boccaccio actually intended to write two versions of the work. (For Lodovico Bartoli's version of the *Corbaccio* in *ottava rima*—fulfilling this "promise"—see the same note in Cassell's edition.) A passage a few lines away gives us a clue to Boccaccio's lack of seriousness in suggesting that there will be an eventual verse *Corbaccio*: "Ora, io non so, se animo non si muta, la nostra città avrà un buon tempo poco che cantare altro che delle sue miserie e cattività, senza che io m'ingegnerò con più perpetuo verso testimonianza delle sue malvage e disoneste opere lasciare a' futuri" [Now I do not know: unless I change my mind, our city shall have {little} to sing about besides its misfortunes and wretchedness for a while—unless, that is, I exert myself to leave to future generations witness of her wicked and indecent acts in the more lasting form of verse] (535). The entire sentence is difficult to grasp, especially its first half, but its concluding clause (which Cassell mistranslates as follows: "moreover, I will strive to leave testimony about her wicked and indecent acts in more lasting verse to those yet to come") suggests that the narrator will eventually compose a verse version of his vituperation of his former beloved. When we remember his earlier disdain for the metrical letter sent him by the widow, we may wonder at his own poetic ambitions. And we also remember that we are reading the prose redaction of the promised poetic treatment. Boccaccio is surely pulling our leg.

28. He shows that he follows his own precepts from the first lines of the text: "Qualunque persona, tacendo, i benefici ricevuti nasconde . . . dimostra sé essere ingrato. . . ." [Whoever . . . hides benefits he has received by being silent . . . shows himself ungrateful . . .]. No ingrate he.

29. When we remember the similar requests of some of Dante's Purgatorial acquaintances—none marked by allusion to cash transactions—we see the further point of Boccaccio's generic allusion to such moments in Dante's poem—and to the comic distortion lent by the detail in this context.

30. The allusion to the disappearance of Virgil in *Purgatorio* XXX is patent, especially in light of the studding of allusions to the *Commedia* in these passages: eight between §551 and §555 (see Appendix 1).

31. In this particular, too, he resembles the narrator of the *Decameron*: ". . . ora che libero dir mi posso" (*Proemio*, 7), who has similarly been freed from the bonds of love by the *consolazione* offered by *alcun amico* (*Proemio*, 4). See Appendix 2 for other points of contact between the narrators of the two works.

32. It is perhaps impossible not to hear the echo of the conclusion of the *Vita*

Notes

Nuova in these words: ". . . io spero di dicer di lei quello che mai non fue detto d'alcuna" [I hope to say of her what has never been said of any woman] (XLII, 2), as has previously been noted by Lopriore (1956): 486.

33. Cf. *Remedia amoris*, 655–658, verses also cited by Cassell (1974, 68 and 1975, xxiv), to a similar end:

> Sed modo dilectam scelus est odisse puellam:
> Exitus ingeniis convenit iste feris.
> Non curare sat est: odio qui finit amorem,
> Aut amat, aut aegre desinet esse miser.
>
> [But to hate a woman once loved is a crime: that is an end fitting to savage minds. It is enough to be indifferent: he who ends love by hating, either loves still, or will find it hard to end his misery.] (trans. J. H. Mozley)

It is difficult to imagine a former lover possessed of a more *ferum ingenium* than our narrator.

34. See Hollander (1977), 100–02, for a brief analysis of these *congedi*.

35. Cassell's text mistranslates the first of the final two sentences as follows: "She is to be stung by the sharpest goad you bear with you." In a letter to me of 26 June 1987 he has emended his translation as it now appears, above. (Bergin's translation of the passage [1981, 199] is similarly flawed.)

36. See the final item in Appendix 1, a rapprochement previously suggested by Pinelli (1883 : 171).

37. *Decameron* I, Intro., 49, 51: she is twenty-eight years old, and thus, we might choose to consider, the only member of the *brigata* to have been born while Dante was still alive (1320). See *Tutte le opere di Giovanni Boccaccio*, vol. 4, *Decameron*, ed. Vittore Branca (Milan: Mondadori, 1976), 19–20. All citations of the *Decameron* are from this edition.

38. Branca, *Opere* 4 : 1430, locates the beginning of this tradition in two sixteenth-century figures, Luigi Groto and Francesco Sansovino. Padoan (1978, 202) refers to Ludovico Dolce's life of Boccaccio, dating from the same century, which sanctions the notion that it was poor Giovanni himself who was left out in the snow, thus occasioning the revenge on the lady taken in the *Corbaccio*. Padoan adds that this basic hypothesis, as recently as 1900, lies behind E. Rossi's conjecture that the *Corbaccio* was written before the *Decameron* was completed.

39. Dioneo, "king" of Day VII, had selected the *beffe* played by wives on their husbands as the subject for that day's story-telling; Lauretta, "queen" of Day VIII, denies the temptation to pay him back by making that Day's theme the obverse, and settles for a sexually undetermined series of tales: "quelle beffe che tutto il giorno o donna a uomo o uomo a donna o l'uno uomo all'altro si fanno" [those tricks which every day are played, whether by woman on man, man on woman, or one man on another] (VII, Conc., 3). I will return to this passage later. For a study of the rubrics of the *Decameron* which points out that they are far from being adequately representative of the deeper concerns of Boccaccio's fiction, see Antonio D'Andrea, "Le rubriche del *Decameron*," *Yearbook of Italian Studies* 2–3 (1973–75 [1976]): 41–67.

40. See Branca, *Opere* 4 : 1431, for the same view. Boccaccio may also have remembered Dante's presentation of Helen in *Inferno* V, 64, "Elena vidi, per cui

tanto reo tempo si volse" [Behold Helen, for whose sake so many woeful years went by].

41. Thus, if he is not Paride, he has come home to Florence from Parigi. Marcus (1984, 28) assigns to Paris the role, within the tale, of being a center for *amour courtois*. My own view is more traditional; its role as center of scholastic instruction is of greater importance in the context of this *novella*.

42. Here and elsewhere the parallels with the *Corbaccio*, which are amply documented throughout Cassell's notes to his translation, are fairly striking—as are the differences: Elena, for instance, is in fact beautiful; Rinieri's sexual urges and appreciations are genuinely felt. Their youth creates another set of problems than that created by the relative age of the odd couple in the later work.

43. The notion that he might possess such abilities is first introduced by her maid (47), thus in part removing at least some of the pretext for pity which we might otherwise feel urged to experience when she breaks her leg in her fall from the tower (142).

44. We can here hardly forget the first line of the *Decameron:* "Umana cosa è aver compassione degli afflitti" [It is human to feel compassion for the afflicted]. Robert M. Durling has noted the implicit criticism of the protagonist's actions offered by this sentence; see "A Long Day in the Sun: *Decameron* 8.7," in *Shakespeare's "Rough Magic": Renaissance Essays in Honor of C. L. Barber*, ed. P. Erickson and C. Kahn (Newark: University of Delaware Press, 1985), 274. Durling also suggests that this *novella* draws on Dante's *rime petrose*, especially "Io son venuto" and "Così nel mio parlar" (for the latter's reflection in the *Corbaccio*, see the citation following n. 36 in the text, above). For speculation on a possible reference to the opening of Horace's *Ars poetica* in Boccaccio's beginning, see Hollander (1985–86), 216n. The inner struggle in Rinieri might be expressed in terms of a choice between a Horatian and a Juvenalian revenge, in which the latter triumphs overwhelmingly.

45. We may remember the reminiscence of Cato at the appearance of the guide in the narrator's dream (*Corbaccio*, 67). See n. 13, above.

46. For his phrase "e mille lacciuoli col mostrar d'amarti t'aveva tesi intorno a' piedi . . ." [and the thousand snares, when I feigned I loved you, that I had twined around your feet] (98) echoes *Inferno* XXII, 109, Dante's description of Ciampolo, who "avea lacciuoli a gran divizia" [possessed snares in great abundance]. That the widow has learned nothing—at least not in the moral sense—by the end of the *novella* is underscored when she is described as still having "a gran divizia lacciuoli" (146). Castelvetro long ago (1570) noted this second resonance of Dante's phrase in his commentary to that canto which itself records such fierce *vendetta*. See also Bettinzoli (1983–84), 224 (see n. 97, below).

47. Marcus (1984), 35–36 notices both the shift from first to second person plural and the scholar's taking on of another identity.

48. We have no indication whatever that such is the case and must therefore suppose that the boast is made only to wound.

49. It seems to me no accident that, of the twenty-four uses of the noun *vendetta* in the *Decameron*, fully ten occur in VIII, 7: 3, 40, 78, 80, 86, 87 (twice), 97, 100, 148; that six of the nineteen occurrences of the verb *vendicare* do also: 70, 77, 79, 88, 93, 122. *Vendetta* is the key word, or concept, of this work and, in my opinion, of the later *Corbaccio*.

Notes

50. (Italics added.) *Riardere* is a hapax in the *Decameron* and occurs only once else in the *Commedia*, at *Purgatorio* XXVII, 4. I might add that Rinieri's name, while I am sure it may be found amply enough in other sources (and it occurs twice in *Inferno* XII, 137), also happens to occur in *Purgatorio* XIV, 88–89, where another Rinieri, a former victim of the sin of envy, is presented as "'l pregio e l'onore/de la casa da Calboli" [praise and honor of the house of Calboli].

51. This citation has been noted by Attilio Bettinzoli (1981–82), 286. I would add that in both works the word is a hapax.

52. I agree almost entirely with Marcus's characterization of Boccaccio's motives in writing the *novella* (1984, 27): "It is as if *Decameron* VIII, 7, were written to show Boccaccio's detractors what kind of writing their criticisms of secular love literature would produce, where erotic desire is transformed into antifeminist {anti-female?} rage and futile poetic invention gives way to sterile invective." Where we differ is also apparent from her response to Barricelli's (1975) proposal that the *Corbaccio* is to be taken ironically. She is not, she says, convinced that Barricelli has proven the existence of what she calls an "ironic split" between author and narrator: "There seems to be no Archimedean point outside the text which could afford the author {reader?} a superior critical perspective, nor any alternative system of values to replace the flawed one that led Giovanni into the *laberinto d'amore*" (40n.). (The trace of the view of the *Corbaccio* as autobiography makes this formulation suspect to this reader.) I am suggesting that *Decameron* VIII, 7, itself offers some such external point from which we should observe the behavior of the narrator of the *Corbaccio*. And I will shortly suggest that the figure of Ovid offers still another external point from which we may examine the text in a better light.

53. See Hollander (1977), 174.

54. See esp. 20–30, 139–48.

55. Fundamental in stemming the tide of modernist readings remains Vittore Branca, *Boccaccio medievale e nuovi studi sul "Decameron,"* 5th ed. (Florence: Sansoni, 1981).

56. It is for this reason that I have constantly insisted, perhaps risking the reader's impatience, on referring to the main first-person voice we hear in the *Corbaccio* as belonging to its "narrator" and not to its author. The former term is meant to confer no independent existence beyond the confines of the work.

57. If I no longer take as seriously as I once did these apparent "orthodox" resolutions of human desire, seeing them rather as playful and ironic, I remain disturbed by the views of those who maintain that the Boccaccio of the *opere minori* is simply not aware of his own aims. See, for instance, the opinion of Robert Hastings (1975), 64: "In the *Amorosa Visione* and the *Ninfale d'Ameto*, where Boccaccio still feels the need to pay lip service to the traditional morality of the medieval Church, the contradiction between the expressed ascetic ideal and the blatantly mundane and sensual interests of the author would strike the reader as mere hypocrisy, were the effects not so unintentionally comical."

58. See Padoan (1963) and (1978), and also Marti (1976). The third section of Appendix 3 gives a quick overview of the state of the debate as it currently exists.

59. Marti (1976), 63–71, while coming back to Manni's "autobiographical" reading of §179, gives Padoan his basic hypothesis by arguing for an "ideal date" (cf. Dante's 1300 for the *Commedia*) of the *action* of the *Corbaccio*, and for a later date of composition (1363–66). Such a theory supports the basic point of Padoan's

argument: that the work was written after Boccaccio's "conversion" in 1362. For my own (negative) view of the putative conversion, see Hollander (1977), 121–23, 236–37. And now see Iovino (1983), 10–88, for a vigorous attack upon those who posit a "spiritual crisis" as an explanation for the (supposed) misogyny of the *Corbaccio*. Her attack, which is principally aimed at Padoan and Branca, makes a number of important and telling points, perhaps the most important being that Boccaccio's removal from Florence to Certaldo (1361?) and subsequent return (1365) were both far more likely to have been motivated by political than religious concerns. She also points out that none of the sixteen early biographers of Boccaccio discuss the return to Certaldo in ways that would authorize a "conversion theory," which would first be put forward by Foscolo only in 1826.

60. In light of such remarks, it is difficult to accept the characterization offered by Marti (1976, 64) of Padoan's procedures: "In verità egli propone quest' ipotesi con grande cautela e prudenza . . ." [In truth he puts forward this hypothesis with great caution and care . . .].

61. For Cassell's unanswered objections to Padoan's "internal evidence" that the work is late, see the following notes in his translation: 87, 231, 299.

62. See n. 8, above, for the references and for the other item mentioned there.

63. See Hollander (1977), 141–42, in part reproduced in Appendix 2.

64. Here, I disagree with Marti (1976), 79, who argues that the *Corbaccio* is much closer in spirit to Dante's *Commedia* (than to the *Decameron*), "come *fictio* potentemente allegorica di valori morali tradizionali" [as a powerfully allegorical fiction marked by traditional moral values]. Further, see Padoan's (1978:208) own keen appreciation of the cunning references (§§229–30) made by Boccaccio in the *Corbaccio* to *novelle* II, 10; IV, 10; V, 10; VII, 5; VII, 9.

65. *Opere*, 4:1198.

66. We should pause to reflect that we have been given the spirit-guide's approximate age at §67: ". . . gli anni, de' quali sessanta o forse più dimostrava d'avere . . ." [. . . his age—which seemed to be sixty or perhaps more . . .]. Since we know *his* age, do we not come to §179 still expecting to be given similar information about our "hero"? It is difficult to find fault with the traditional reading of the passage, which descends from Manni (1742). And we might go on to consider that the situation which serves as pretext for the *Decameron* itself is in fact carefully dated (I, Intro., 8): 1348. In that instance, a gap of approximately five years is presented in the text. Here, we have no such extended period of separation between event and narration, as I will presently argue.

67. The *Corbaccio*'s narrator's notable departure from earlier Boccaccian narrators in celebrating as his lady the Blessed Virgin rather than that other "Mary," Maria d'Aquino or "Fiammetta," should probably be considered more cautiously than it tends to be.

68. ". . . ciascun luogo della nostra città, qual che si fosse più di litigi e di quistioni pieno, m'incominciò a parere più qieto e più riposato che la mia casa" [. . . our city, however full it was of quarrels and disputes, began to seem quieter and more peaceful to me than my house].

69. Several scholars have challenged both these points regarding dating. See Cassell (1975), nn. 231, 299.

70. Padoan (1978, 207). On the other hand, he goes on to claim that misogynist moments found in the *Filocolo* and *Decameron* are "solo accenni del tutto tradizionali" [only entirely traditional references]. This partial opening to what

Notes

might have been a wider discussion fails to account for still other misogynist moments in Boccaccio's *oeuvre*, as well as for "misandrogynist" ones. The war between men and women, from the *Caccia di Diana* on, is a constant feature of Boccaccian narrative and draws with it outbursts against the other sex each time a speaker, whether male or female, is thwarted in his or her desire or feels betrayed. More importantly, Padoan's view does not allow for the possibility that the misogyny of the *Corbaccio* is itself "traditional," that it does not necessarily require the "enthusiastic adhesion" of its author.

71. If we examine the single most misogynist text in Boccaccio's final work, one of the last passages, probably, that Boccaccio wrote (*Esposizioni, Inferno* XVI, esp. litt. 27–46), we find ourselves confronted with a "little *Corbaccio*." Explaining the cause of Iacopo Rusticucci's turning to men as sexual partners, and thus to the cause of his eternal damnation, Boccaccio tells us that it was Iacopo's shrewish wife who caused him to turn to homosexuality for his sexual pleasure. The four-page tirade that follows, which begins by warning men to be extremely careful before taking a wife, ends by claiming, on the basis of what Boccaccio has often heard, that women may look like angels when one sees them on the street in the daylight, but that at night they are demons in bed. In between we find references to the authority of Jerome and Theophrastus in these matters, and many of the indictments of women which we find in the *Corbaccio*. Whatever else the passage represents, it is surely to be regarded as "traditional" misogyny. How seriously are we to take it? That is more difficult to say. It may be heartfelt (Boccaccio, who never married and sired five children, was perhaps inclined to love and despise women at almost the same moment); it may be a conventional rhetorical display. When we examine the occasion for the outburst, Iacopo's turning to homosexuality, we may consider that Boccaccio had pierced to the heart of the matter of misogynist literature, which must have been often precisely the weapon wielded by homosexual clerics *contra feminas* and thus as *apologia pro moribus suis*. In any case, the occasion for the outburst is a suspect one. And I, for one, do not think even the authority of Dante, who sanctions Boccaccio's analysis of the causes for Iacopo's homosexuality, could really convince Boccaccio any more than it can convince me that a shrewish wife is sufficient cause for turning one's carnal appetite to one's own sex. There are always other women to turn to—as Boccaccio knew at least as well as anyone else.

72. For recent contributions, as well as discussions of earlier proposals, see Cassell (1970), Cottino-Jones (1970), Cartier (1975), Marti (1976, 60–63), Hollander (1977, 139–40), Padoan (1978, 224n.–225n.).

73. See especially Marti's felicitous observations of details in the text which suggest crow-like attributes in the widow's behavior (1976, 60–62). For a brief listing of some of those who believe that the title refers essentially or only to the widow, see Appendix 3, item 6. Iovino (1983:222–23) believes that it refers to the husband.

74. In this particular I followed Nurmela (1968), 16–17.

75. Dioneo's self-description as a "black crow" (*nero corvo*) among the *brigata* of "white doves" (*Decameron* IX, x, 3) has received some attention in discussions of the title of the *Corbaccio*. (Lauren Scancarelli Seem, a graduate student at Princeton, has called my attention to the possible resonance of Ovid's presentation of the cause of the raven's being turned from white to black in *Metamorphoses*

2.531–632 both in this passage and in the title of the *Corbaccio*. His crow is punished for revealing the unchaste behavior of the maid Coronis to Apollo.) I would suggest that, as the controlling presence among the ten narrators of the *Decameron*, the one who tells the most disturbing truths and who insists upon their truthful painfulness, Dioneo has something of the role of the narrator of the *Corbaccio*. Yet I believe that Boccaccio basically aligns himself with Dioneo and against his own alter ego in the following work. It is my view (one that obviously cannot be developed in this circumstance) that his Dioneo is presented as disinterested in his attempt to get the others of the *brigata* to understand their natures, while the narrator of the *Corbaccio* is put forward as an interested party in an unsavory *vendetta*.

76. Paul Watson, "An Immodest Proposal Concerning the *Corbaccio*," forthcoming in *Studi sul Boccaccio*, 16 (1987–88), n. 21. I thank Professor Watson for having sent me a typescript of his paper, as well as the galleys of the resulting article. He argues interestingly, on the basis of a Florentine illumination found in a codex of 1450 (Bib. Naz., Pal. Bald. 156), at the left margin of the incipit, that the illuminator equated an apparently speaking crow with the book or perhaps with Boccaccio himself. Watson does not overrule the previous identification of widow and crow, but lends support to this second meaning, arguing that several details in the text associate the narrator with birds and their behaviors. He adds, on the evidence of the *Fior di virtù*, a fourteenth-century bestiary, that black crows are also identified with sadness, indeed with *malinconia*, the child of madness, and thus are appropriate emblems for our narrator.

77. For confirmation of these facts, see Padoan's note to the *Esposizioni*, *Inferno* IV, esp. litt., 122 (p. 829 in *Opere*, vol. 6). The *Ibis*, though not one of Ovid's better-known texts in the Middle Age, was known by others, including several of Boccaccio's predecessors. See Roberto Weiss, *Il primo secolo dell'umanesimo* (Rome: Edizioni di "Storia e Letteratura," 1949), 37 (for Geremia da Montagnone, ca. 1260–1321); Guido Billanovich, "«*Veterum vestigia vatum*» nei carmi dei preumanisti padovani," *Italia medioevale e umanistica* 1 (1958): 231–32 (for Lovato and Mussato as citers of the *Ibis*—with nine citations between them); A. Teresa Hankey, "The Library of Domenico di Bandino [1335?–1418]," *Rinascimento* 8 (1957): 184.

78. For the tradition of the literary curse—a form of spell—see the appendix (pp. 359–72) in J. H. Mozley's edition of Ovid in the Loeb Classics series, *The "Art of Love" and Other Poems* (1929; reprint, Cambridge, Mass.: Harvard University Press, London: Heinemann, 1969). (Citations of Ovid's texts are drawn from this edition.) And for a study of the satirical element in Cervantes, see Alban Forcione, *Cervantes and the Mystery of Lawlessness* (Princeton: Princeton University Press, 1984). The introduction (pp. 13–18) contains many points which are relevant to a consideration of the satirical impulse in Boccaccio.

79. Ovid's care in dating his own work (cf., again, §179 of the *Corbaccio*) and his outraged sense that his reputation is being besmirched by a *maldicente*—in both works the cause for writing is precisely bad-mouthing of the author by an enemy—are two similarities shared by *Corbaccio* and *Ibis*.

80. Boccaccio's knowledge of the *Ibis* would indicate that he is aware, through it, of the very origin of wounding satire in the distant figure of Callimachus.

Notes

81. *Ibis.*, 639–44:

> Haec tibi tantisper subito sint missa libello,
> Inmemores ne nos esse querare tui.
> Pauca quidem, fateor: sed di dent plura rogatis,
> Multiplicentque suo vota favore mea.
> Postmodo plura leges et nomen habentia verum,
> Et pede quo debent acria bella geri.

82. I speak of model rather than source. Juvenal's sixth *Satire*, as has long been recognized, serves as source for many of the misogynous passages in the *Corbaccio*, as the notes in Nurmela's edition and Cassell's translation make plain. See also Nardo (1979). For an early (and lengthy) recognition of the relation between these two texts, see Pinelli (1883), 178–91.

83. Beginning with Billanovich (1947), 161–62. See also, among others, Padoan (1963); 11n., (1964), 199, (1978), 210; Cassell (1974), 68; Hollander (1977), 28, 147, 148; Nardo (1979), 252; Nykrog (1984), 440; Smarr (1986), 155–56, 162–63.

84. See Hollander (1977, 112–16) for an attempt to show how deeply Boccaccio's debt to the Ovidian persona affected his work. I now find myself disagreeing with many of the formulations in that treatment, if not its central point.

85. I have already treated the fairly obvious citation of the *Remedia amoris* in the *Decameron* (see Hollander [1985–86, 216] and have done so again in my forthcoming study of the *Proemio*. Ovid, having offered his *remedia*, advice which would keep us from jealous desires for perfidious mistresses, adds two final bits of medicinal wisdom concerning which foods to ingest and which to shun and how to regulate our consumption of wine (either none or too much). His words describing his dietary laws ("quos fugias quosque sequare"—796) are the most probable source for Boccaccio's phrase "quello che sia da fuggire e che sia similmente da seguitare" [that which is to be shunned and, likewise, to be sought] (*Decameron*, Pr. 14). In the first essay referred to above, I also had this to say concerning the verses which immediately follow the Ovidian text just cited: "Ovid goes on, with a wry dead-pan shot at the opening lines of the *Aeneid*, to single out the onion as a food to be avoided: 'Daunius, an Libycis bulbus tibi missus ab oris / An veniat Megaris, noxius omnis erit' [Onions, whether Italian or sent from Libya's shores or arriving from Megara, every one of them will be harmful] 797–98). The *bulbus daunius* might have struck Boccaccio as a fitting emblem for the food of love; it is his own 'emblem', that 'Italian onion' which was the main product of Certaldo" (216n.). Boccaccio finds the chief agricultural product of his hometown presented as the "food of love" in Ovid's verses, and surely must have smiled in recognition.

86. See Hollander (1977), 144, citing *Esposizioni*, *Inferno* XIII (151: "Io fei gibbetto a me de le mie case" [I made my house a gibbet for myself]), esp. litt., 113.

87. Boccaccio uses the noun *trave* once in the *Corbaccio* (it does not occur in the *Decameron*): "Tanto t'è per lei prenderli, quanto se per una delle travi della tua camera li prendessi" [It is the same for you to do this {suffer} for her as to do it for one of the beams in your room] (40). While the immediate context only serves to equate the unfeeling widow with similarly insentient wood, the larger

context—an intended suicide by hanging, probably from exactly that beam—may indicate that Boccaccio was thinking of the suicidal disappointed lover in Ovid's poem, hanging *a trabe*.

88. And for information regarding the emergence of the *Remedia* as a school-text in the twelfth through fourteenth centuries, see Ralph J. Hexter, *Ovid and Medieval Schooling* (Munich: Arbeo-Gesellschaft, 1968), esp. 15–21. Hexter's book is a mine of new information concerning the medieval tradition of Ovidian texts.

89. See n. 83, above, for an indication of some of the discussions of this relationship.

90. See my previous discussion of this matter, Hollander (1977), 114.

91. Boccaccio's text also is a "little book": "piccola mia operetta" (560). For Boccaccio's covert reference to the *Amores* when he describes his own *novelle* as being "senza titolo" (*Decameron* IV, Introduction, 3) see Hollander (1977), 115–16. The second half of the first verse of the *Remedia* (". . . titulum nomenque libelli" [the name and title of this little book]) tells us that Ovid meant by *titulum* more than the title of a work. The word would, in fact, seem to indicate what we today refer to as "title page," i.e., the name, author's name, and/or other indications found before the text actually begins.

92. See esp. *Decameron* IV, Intro., 5; X, Conc. Aut., 3.

93. The brilliant and only apparently self-effacing opening of the fourth Day (*Decameron* IV, Intro, 2–4) adroitly attributes invidious sentiments to all his detractors.

94. It is interesting to consider that, when he does turn to satire, in the *Ibis*, Ovid continues to use elegiacs and not iambics.

95. The passage must surely have struck Dante. In the *Commedia* he is the "Ovid" who may seek successfully to rival Virgil. For Boccaccio, the comparison would rather be between himself as "Ovid" and Dante as "Virgil," with the additional advantage to himself being that he has written "true" epic where Dante had not—even by his own admission in *De vulg. Eloq.* See my study "Dante and the Martial Epic," forthcoming in the Festschrift for Aldo S. Bernardo (Binghamton, N.Y.: Medieval and Renaissance Texts and Studies, 1988[?]).

96. Particularly important is the first section of the *Remedia* (1–218). See, again, my forthcoming study of the *Proemio*, from which I have borrowed Appendix 4, which gives a sense of the extent of Boccaccio's interest in Ovid's text.

97. See Delcorno (1979). It is important to note that, with the single and perhaps not imposing exception of Levi's (1889), there are no studies before Delcorno's dedicated to any of Boccaccio's fictions which relate them centrally to Dante's texts. The subject has been treated partially and fitfully, despite its obvious importance. Other recent works which are specifically concerned with the presence of Dantean text in Boccaccio's work, all, with the exception of the last, published in *Studi sul Boccaccio*, include: Hollander (1981–82); Bettinzoli (1981–82), continued under the same title in the following volume, 14 (1983–84); Hollander, "The Sun Rises in Dante," *Studi sul Boccaccio* 14 (1983–84):241–55; "Boccaccio's Dante," *Italica* 63 (1986):278–89. On the other hand, there is a large amount of material which deals with the more focused issue of Boccaccio's response to Dante in the works which he devoted to his precursor. For a survey and bibliography, see Padoan, "Boccaccio, Giovanni," *Enciclopedia dantesca* I

Notes

(Rome: Istituto della Enciclopedia Italiana, 1965):645–50; and for additional bibliography, see Hollander (1981–82), 170n.

98. The preceding moment, in which he finds himself bathed in sweat, "tutto di sudore bagnato" [bathed all over in sweat] (555), reflects a similarly solemn moment of transition from realm to realm in Dante, this time the crossing of Acheron (*Inferno* III, 132): "la mente di sudore ancor mi bagna" [my mind yet again bathes me in sweat].

99. For some recent penetrating thought about the tactics of citation in classical Latin texts, see Gian Biagio Conte, *The Rhetoric of Imitation*, trans. Charles Segal (Ithaca and London: Cornell University Press, 1986).

100. Margherita Frankel, who read the manuscript of this essay, has offered several observations which I am particularly pleased to share: §69: "paura mi porse," *Inferno* I, 52–53: "mi prose tanto di gravezza / con la paura . . ."; §74: "Come ci se' tu venuto? Qual tracutanza t'ha qui guidato?," *Purgatorio* I, 43: "Chi v'ha guidati?"; §532: "a niuno mio successore lascerò a far delle ingiurie . . . vendetta," *Paradiso* XXX, 34–35: "io la lascio a maggior bando / che quel de la mia tuba"; §532: "solo che tanto tempo mi sia prestato," *Vita Nuova* XLII, 2: ". . . che la mia vita duri alquanti anni, io spero di dicer di lei . . ."; §537: "perché più tosto a te che ad alcun altro di quelli fu questa fatica imposta?" *Par.* XXI, 77–78: "perché predestinata fosti sola / a questo officio tra le tue consorte."

101. Nykrog (1984) agrees with this view of the *Corbaccio*, but, not being a *boccaccista*, developed his interpretation without benefit of our in-house squabbles.

Appendix 1:

TEXTS IN THE *CORBACCIO* REFLECTING PASSAGES IN DANTE

Some of these confrontations are more speculative than others; many more might still have been suggested—indeed some have been. Passages in Dante referred to by Pier Giorgio Ricci (in his notes to his edition of 1965), Tauno Nurmela (1968), Mario Marti (1972), and Anthony K. Cassell (1975) are marked with the appropriate parenthetic initials (PGR, TN, MM, AKC). The essential study to be consulted remains the brief pamphlet by Attilio Levi, "*Il Corbaccio*" *e* "*La Divina Commedia*": *note e raffronti* (Turin: E. Loescher, 1889). Levi's contributions, which are not all as convincing as some, are indicated by L.

Il Corbaccio:	Dante:
§1: Qualunque persona, tacendo, i benefici ricevuti nasconde senza di ciò aver cagione convenevole, secondo il mio giudicio assai manifestamente dimostra sé essere ingrato e mal conoscente di quegli.	*Par.* XVII, 85–88, 91–92: Le sue magnificenze conosciute saranno ancora sì che' suoi nemici non ne potran tener le lingue mute. A lui t'aspetta e a' suoi benefici . . . e portera'ne scritto ne la mente di lui, e nol dirai; . . .
§2: . . . il fonte secca della pietà!	*Mon.* II, v, 5 & *Ep.* V, 7 (PGR, AKC): Romanum imperium de Fonte nascitur pietatis. . . . cum sit Caesar et maiestas eius de Fonte defluat pietatis.
§3: . . . nell'umile trattato . . .	*Inf.* I, 8: ma per trattar del ben ch'io vi trovai
§3: . . . ma per sola benignità di Colei	*Par.* XXXIII, 34–35 (AKC), 36–37: Ancor ti priego, regina, che puoi

Appendix 1

che impetrandola di Colui che vuol quello ch'Ella medesima, . . .

(And see §120 for PGR's citation of the passage.)

§4:
La qual cosa faccendo, non solamente parte del mio dovere pagherò, ma senza niun dubbio potrò a molti lettori di quella fare utilità.

§5:
. . . priego Colui . . . che alla presente opera della sua luce siffattamente illumini il mio intelletto. . . .

§12:
. . . me, in così fatta battaglia dimorante, . . .

§42:
. . . tuo folle amor . . .

§47:
. . . dagli occhi della mente . . .

§54:
. . . in altissimo sonno legato . . .

§54:
. . . mia nimica fortuna

§54:
e davanti alla virtù fantastica, la quale il sonno non lega, diverse forme paratemi, . . .

§58:
. . . una nebbia sì folta e sì oscura . . .

ciò che tu vuoli, che conservi sani, dopo tanto veder, li affetti suoi.
Vinca tua guardia i movimenti umani:

Par. XXXII, 145–148:
Veramente, *ne* forse tu t'arretri
 movendo l'ali tue, credendo oltrarti,
orando grazia conven che s'impetri
grazia da quella che puote aiutarti;

Purg. X, 106–108:
Non vo' però, lettor, che tu ti smaghi
 di buon proponimento per udire
 come Dio vuol che 'l debito si paghi.

Par. IV, 124–126:
Io veggio ben che già mai non si sazia
nostro intelletto, se 'l ver non lo illustra
di fuor dal qual nessun vero si spazia.

VN XIV, 1 (AKC):
. . . la battaglia de li diversi pensieri . . .

Par. VIII, 2–3:
la bella Ciprigna il folle amor raggiasse . . .

Purg. X, 122 (L, AKC):
. . . de la vista de la mente . . .

Purg. XV, 119 (L):
. . . dal sonno si slega,

Inf. II, 61:
l'amico mio, e non de la ventura,

Purg. XVII, 1–45, esp. 22–24:
e qui fu la mia mente sì ristretta
dentro da sé, che di fuor non venìa
cosa che fosse allor da lei ricetta.

Purg. XV, 142–143 (AKC & see XVII, 2):
Ed ecco a poco a poco un fummo farsi
verso di noi come la notte oscuro;

Texts Reflecting Passages in Dante

§59:
... speranza ... all'entrare del cammino mi fece cadere.

Inf. II, 142:
intrai per lo cammino alto e silvestro.

§61:
... in una solitudine diserta, aspra e fiera, piena di salvatiche piante, ...

Inf. I, 5 (L, TN, AKC):
esta selva selvaggia e aspra e forte

§61:
... di pruni e di bronchi ...

Inf. XIII, 26 (PGR, TN):
... tante voci uscisser, tra quei bronchi,
(And for *pruno*, see XIII, 32.)

§62:
... né conoscere da qual parte io mi fossi in quella entrato;

Inf. I, 10 (L):
Io non so ben ridir com'i' v'intrai,

§63:
... dove che io mi volgessi,

Inf. VI, 6 (L):
... ch'io mi volga,

§63:
... sentire mugghi, urli e strida di diversi e ferocissimi animali, ...

Inf. V, 29, 35:
che mugghia come fa mar per tempesta ...
quivi le strida, il compianto ...

(And see Dante's similar confusion in *Inf.* XIII, where he thinks the sinners are hiding behind the thornbushes, which in fact they have become, as here the narrator takes the lovers for beasts, a passage alluded to again at §124.)

§66:
... da ogni speranza abbandonato

Inf. III, 9:
LASCIATE OGNE SPERANZA ...

§66–67:
e ecco, ... venir verso me con lento passo un uomo senza alcuna compagnia. ... era di statura grande, di pelle e di pelo bruno, benché in parte bianco divenuto fosse per gli anni, ...

Purg. I, 31–36:
vidi presso di me un veglio solo,
   degno di tanta reverenza in vista,
   che più non dee a padre alcun figliuolo.
Lunga la barba e di pel bianco mista
   portava, a' suoi capelli simigliante,
   de' quai cadeva al petto doppia lista.

§66:
... nella misera valle ...
(And see §556.)

Purg. XIV, 41:
li abitator de la misera valle

§71:
... se in lui fia spirito di pietà alcuno, ...

Inf. XIII, 36 (L, PGR, MM, AKC):
non hai tu spirto di pietade alcuno?

§72:
E mentre che io in così fatto pensiere dimorava, esso, senza ancora dire alcuna cosa, ...

Inf. I, 61–63:
Mentre ch'i' rovinava in basso loco,
   dinanzi agli occhi mi si fu offerto
   chi per lungo silenzio parea fioco.

Appendix 1

§72:
... immaginando se io per quello [nome], misericordia e aiuto chiedendogli, il nominassi, ... con maggiore e più pronta affezione a' miei bisogni il dovessi muovere.

Inf. I, 65–66, 79–80:
"*Miserere* di me," gridai a lui,
"qual che tu sii, od ombra od omo certo!"
Or se' tu quel Virgilio e quella fonte
che spandi di parlar sì largo fiume?

§73:
... per lo mio proprio nome chiamando ...

Purg. XXX, 55:
"Dante, ..."

§74:
Qual malvagia fortuna, qual malvagio destino ...?

Inf. XV, 46: XXXII, 76 (L, MM):
... Qual fortuna o destino
se voler fu o destino o fortuna,

§75:
Io, costui udendo, e parendomi nel suo sembiante di me pietoso, prima che io potessi alla risposta avere la voce, dirottamente, di me stesso increscendomi, a piagnere incominciai.

Purg. XXX, 94–99:
ma poi che 'ntesi ne le dolci tempre
   lor compartire* a me, par che se detto
avesser: "Donna, perché sì lo stempre?",
lo gel che m'era intorno al cor ristretto,
spirito e acqua fessi, e con angoscia
   de la bocca e de li occhi uscì del petto.

(*This confrontation would suggest that Boccaccio's text of the *Commedia* registered the more common reading, "compatire.")

§77:
... il falso piacere delle caduche cose ... m'ebbe menato,

Purg. XXXI, 34–35 (L, AKC):
Le presenti cose
col falso lor piacer volser miei passi, ...

§78:
... io ti priego ... per quello Iddio per lo quale ogni cosa si dee, ... m' insegni com'io di luogo di tanta paura pieno partir mi possa;

Inf. I, 130–132 (L, AKC):
... io ti richeggio
per quello Dio che tu non conoscesti,
a ciò ch'io fugga questo male e peggio ...

§78:
dalla quale (paura) già sì vinto mi sento che appena conosco se io o vivo o morto mi sono.

Inf. XXXIV, 25:
Io non mori' e non rimasi vivo;

§80:
Veramente mi fa il qui vederti e le tue parole assai manifesto, ...

Inf. X, 25 (L, MM, AKC):
La tua loquela ti fa manifesto ...

§83:
... della vostra mortal vita fui sbandito,

Inf. XV, 81:
de l'umana natura posto in bando;

§83:
... tutti i peli mi si cominciarono ad arricciare;

Inf. XXII, 19–20:
Già mi sentia tutti arriciar li peli
de la paura e stava in dietro intento,

§85:
E di tanto potere fu questa nuova paura, che io non so pensare qual cosa fosse quella che sì forte facesse il mio sonno che egli allora non si rompesse;

Purg. IX, 31–33 (L):
Ivi parea che ella e io ardesse;
e sì lo 'ncendio imaginato cosse,
che convenne che 'l sonno si rompesse.

§89:
... quantunque l'entrare in questo luogo sia apertissimo . . ., egli non è così agevole il riuscirne, . . .

Inf. V, 19–20 (TN, AKC):
guarda com'entri e di cui tu ti fide;
non t'inganni l'ampiezza de l'intrare!

§90:
... né sì subita può essere la nostra partita . . .

Purg. II, 133:
né la nostra partita fu men tosta.

§92:
... o se per se stesso alcuno che c'entri ne può mai uscire;

Inf. IV, 49–50:
uscicci mai alcuno, o per suo merto
o per altrui, che poi fosse beato?

§93:
... e molti "la valle de' sospiri e della miseria";

Inf. V, 118, 123:
... al tempo d'i dolci sospiri,
... nella miseria; ...

§94:
... la morte mi tolse, alla quale tu corri.

Purg. XXXIII, 54:
del viver ch'è un correre a la morte.

§96:
... se Colui che può i tuoi più caldi disii ponga in vera pace, . . .

Par. IV, 115–117 (L, AKC):
Cotal fu l'ondeggiar del santo rio
ch'uscì del fonte ond'ogne ver deriva;
tal puose in pace uno e altro disio.

§98:
... quella prigione etterna . . .

Purg. I, 41, (L, AKC):
... la pregione etterna . . .

§102:
... in quello carcere cieco . . .
(See also §271.)

Inf. X, 58–59 (L, PGR, TN, MM, AKC):
... per questo cieco carcere . . .

§104:
... non è panno manualmente tessuto, anzi è un fuoco dalla divina arte composto, sì fieramente cocente che il vostro è come ghiaccio, a rispetto di questo, freddissimo.

Purg. XXVII, 49–51:
Sì com' fui dentro, in un bogliente vetro
gittato mi sarei per rinfrescarmi,
tant'era ivi lo 'ncendio sanza metro.

Appendix 1

§105:
... alla mia sete tutti vostri fiumi insieme adunati e giù per la mia gola volgendosi sarebbono un piccol sorso.

Inf. XXX, 64–69 (PGR, AKC):
Li ruscelletti che d'i verdi colli
   del Casentin discendon giuso in
     Arno,
facendo i lor canali freddi e molli,
sempre mi stanno innanzi, e non
     indarno,
chè l'imagine lor vie più m'asciuga
che 'l male ond' io nel volto mi
     discarno.

§106:
... di colei la quale tu vorresti d'aver veduta esser digiuno.
(And see §§130 & 534.)

Inf. XXVIII, 86–87 (L, AKC):
e tien la terra che tale qui meco
   vorrebbe di vedere esser di-
     giuno, ...

§108:
... quello infinito Bene ... al quale tutte le cose vivono. ...

VN, XLII, 2 (TN, AKC):
... colui a cui tutte le cose vivono ...

§110:
... il cuore, non altrimenti che faccia la neve al sole, in acqua si risolvesse;

Purg. XXX, 85–87, 97–98:
Sì come neve tra le vive travi
   per lo dosso d'Italia si congela,
   pur che la terra che perde ombra
     spiri, ...
lo gel che m'era intorno al cor
     ristretto,
spirito e acqua fessi, ...

§111:
O bene avventurato spirito,

Par. III, 37 (L, AKC):
O ben creato spirito,

§111:
... le sue etterne bellezze mostrandoci,

Purg. XIV, 149:
mostrandovi le sue bellezze etterne

§115:
... non da umana voce, ma da angelica, ...

Inf. II, 57 (L):
con angelica voce, in sua favella:

§115:
... Colei nel cui ventre si racchiuse la nostra salute ... siccome in termine fisso, ...

Par. XXXIII, 7; 3 (L, PGR, TN, MM, AKC):
Nel ventre tuo si raccese l'amore, ...
termine fisso d'etterno consiglio,

§116:
La qual cosa essendo a' suoi divini occhi manifesta, e veggendoti in questa valle, oltre al modo usato, smarrito e impedito, ...

Inf. II, 61–64 (L):
l'amico mio, e non de la ventura,
   ne la diserta piaggia è impedito
   sì nel cammin, che vòlt' è per
     paura;
e temo che non sia già sì smarrito,

§116: ... uscito di mente, ... (And see §178, where the citation is noted by PGR, TN, MM, & AKC.)	*Purg.* VIII, 15 (MM): che fece me a me uscir di mente;

§116:
... siccome essa benignissima fa assai sovente nelle bisogne de' suoi divoti, che senza priego aspettare da se medesima si muove a sovvenire dell'opportuno aiuto al bisognoso, ...
	Par. XXXIII, 16–18 (L):
	La tua benignità non pur soccorre
	  a chi domanda, ma molte f ïate
	  liberamente al dimandar precorre.

§118: Assai bene m'hai soddisfatto alle mie domande;	*Inf.* X, 126 (L, AKC): E io li sodisfeci al suo dimando.
§118: ... vendetta di Dio è un di nuovo rifarti bello ...	*Purg.* II, 75: quasi obl ïando d'ire a farsi belle.
§118: non al ruinare allo 'nferno,	*Inf.* XX, 35 (AKC?): E non restò di ruinare a valle ... (And see *Inf.* I, 61).
§119: ... la quale per la mia salute t'ha in questa vicenda mandato,	*Purg.* XXX, 51: Virgilio a cui per mia salute die'mi;

§120:
Ma io divotamente Lei priego che può quello ch' ella vuole, ... i miei passi dirizzi alla vita perpetua, e quelli sostenga e conservi ...
	Par. XXXIII, 34–37 (PGR, MM):
	Ancor ti priego, regina, che puoi
	  ciò che tu vuoli, che conservi sani,
	  dopo tanto veder, li affetti suoi.
	Vinca tua guardia i movimenti
	    umani.

§123: ... il raggio de la vera luce ...	*Par.* XXXIII, 53–54: ... lo raggio de l'alta luce che da sé è vera.
§127: Io quasi di mia colpa compunto,	*Inf.* X, 109 (L, PGR, AKC): ... come di mia colpa compunto,

§129:
... io dirci in servigio di te ... che noi a seder ci ponessimo; ma perché qui far non si può, ragioneremo in piede.
	Inf. XV, 37–40 (AKC, citing L):
	"O figliuol," disse, "qual di questa
	    greggia
	s'arresta punto, giace poi cent'anni
	  sanz'arrostarsi quando 'l foco il
	    feggia.
	Però va oltre: i' ti verrò a' panni";

§132: ... come tu dalla nostra vita ti dipartisti, ...	*Inf.* V, 69: ch'amor di nostra vita dipartille.

Appendix 1

§135:
... alcune (donne) nominò della nostra città ... ,

§143:
... il suo viso corse agli occhi miei,

§145:
Deh, guardate come alla cotal donna stanno bene le bende bianche e' panni neri!

§150:
... non altrimenti che faccia su per le cose unte la fiamma,

§155:
Per ciò che io manifestamente conosco (se io celar tel volessi, io non potrei, sì mi pare che tu il vero senta de' fatti miei, donde che tu te l'abbia) niuna cosa te ne nasconderò.

§167:
Forse che il tacerlo sarebbe più onesto;

§168:
e l'anima, che con queste accompagnata soleva essere donna,

§191:
... con altezza d'ingegno ...

§209:
... faccendosi umili, obedienti e blande, le corone, le cinture, i drappi d'oro, i vai, i molti vestimenti e gli altri ornamenti vari, de' quali tutto il

VN, VI, 2:
E presi li nomi di sessanta le più belle donne della cittade ...

Inf. XXIII, 110–111 (L):
... a l'occhio mi corse un, crucifisso ...

Purg. VIII, 73–75 (PGR, TN, AKC):
Non credo che la sua madre più m'ami,
poscia che trasmutò le bianche bende,
le quai convien che, misera!, ancor brami.

Inf. XIX, 28–29 (L, TN, MM, AKC):
Qual suole il fiammeggiar de le cose unte
muoversi pur su per la strema buccia, ...

Inf. X, 100–105 (AKC):
"Noi veggiam, come quei c'ha mala luce,
le cose," disse, "che ne son lontano;
cotanto ancor ne splende il sommo duce.
Quando s'appressano o son, tutto è vano
nostro intelletto; e s'altri non ci apporta,
nulla sapem di vostro stato umano."

Par. XVI, 45 (L, AKC):
più è tacer che ragionare onesto.

Purg. XIX, 51:
ch'avran di consolar l'anime donne.

Inf. X, 59 (L, AKC):
... per altezza d'ingegno,

Purg. XXIII, 98–108 (AKC):
Tempo futuro m'è già nel cospetto,
cui non sarà quest'ora molto antica,

dì si veggono splendenti, da' miseri mariti impetrano; il quale non s'accorge tutte quelle essere armi a combattere la sua signoria e a vincerla.

§218:
Fatti in costà:

§250:
I miseri studianti patiscono i freddi e i digiuni e le vigilie,

§262:
ed è tanta, che fa nel beato regno lieti gli angeli, riguardandola, e a' beati spiriti, se dir si può, aggiugne gloria e maraviglioso diletto.

§268:
... esce di schiera, ...

§269:
... hanno il cammino smarrito,

§278:
... del bene dello 'ntelletto privato non sia, ...

§293:
... assai bene già l'arte dello 'ngannare avendo appresa, ...

§295:
... in Dio me e le cose mie rimettendo.

§306:
... per lo dolce mondo ...

§309:
... della torre della fame ...

ne qual sarà in pergamo interdetto
a le sfacciate donne fiorentine
l'andar mostrando con le poppe il petto.
Quai barbare fuor mai, quai saracine,
cui bisognasse, per farle ir coperte,
o spiritali o altre discipline?
Ma se le svergognate fosser certe
di quel che 'l ciel veloce loro ammanna,
già per urlare avrian le bocche aperte;

Inf. XXII, 96 (TN, AKC):
Fatti 'n costà, malvagio uccello!

Purg. XXIX, 37–38:
O sacrosante Vergini, se fami
freddi o vigilie mai per voi soffersi, ...

Par. XXXI, 133–135 (L, AKC):
Vida a lor giochi quivi e a lor canti
ridere una bellezza, che letizia
era ne li occhi a tutti li altri santi;

Inf. II, 105 (PGR, AKC):
ch'uscì per te de la volgare schiera?

Inf. I, 1–3 (AKC):
Nel mezzo del cammin di nostra vita
mi ritrovai per una selva oscura
ché le diritta via era smarrita.

Inf. III, 18 (PGR, TN, AKC):
c'hanno perduto il ben d'intelletto.

Inf. X, 51 (L):
ma i vostri non appreser ben quell' arte.

Inf. XXII, 51 (L):
distruggitor di sé e di sue cose.

Inf. VI, 88 (L, AKC):
... nel dolce mondo,

Inf. XXXIII, 23 (L, PGR, MM, AKC):
la qual per me ha 'l titol de la fame,

Appendix 1

§312:
... la vernaccia da Corniglio,

§340:
... non altrimenti il falcone tratto di cappello si rifà tutto e sopra sé torna guardandosi, che si faceva ella, ...

§351:
... il mio dovuto amore, ...

§359:
... che Dio t'ami,

§366:
... madonna Cianghella ...

§372:
La sua sete è del digesto che vivi e sani corpi possono senza riaverlo prestare.

§382:
... Galeotto ...

§386:
... quello che tu non puoi aver saputo ...

§398:
... fumo di pantano ...

§405:
... molti ti potessero al mio dire vera testimonianza rendere sì come esperti, a me, ...

§406:
... di due bozzacchioni, che già forse acerbi pomi furono,

§424:
... l'anima mia dal mortal corpo e dalle terrene tenebre sviluppata e sciolta ...

§424:
... vidi e conobbi qual fosse l'animo di questa iniqua e malvagia femmina;

Purg. XXIV, 24 (AKC):
l'anguille di Bolsena e la vernaccia.

Par. XIX, 34–37 (L, TN, AKC):
Quasi falcone ch'esce del cappello,
move la testa e con l'ali si plaude,
voglia mostrando e faccendosi bello,
vid'io farsi quel segno, ...

Inf. XXVI, 95–96 (L, AKC):
... né 'l debito amore
lo qual dovea Penelopè far lieta, ...

Purg. XIII, 146 (L, AKC):
... gran segno è che Dio t'ami;

Par. XV, 128 (L, PGR, MM, TN, AKC):
una Cianghella, ...

Purg. XXV, 43–44 (TN, AKC):
Ancor digesto, scende ov'è più bello tacer che dire; ...

Inf. V, 137 (PGR, AKC):
Galeotto fu 'l libro e chi lo scrisse:

Inf. XXXIII, 19 (PGR):
però quel che non puoi avere inteso,

Inf. VIII, 12 (PGR, TN):
se 'l fummo del pantan nol ti nasconde.

VN, XXVI, 1 (AKC):
e di questo molti, sì come esperti, mi potrebbero testimoniare a chi non lo credesse.

Par. XXVII, 125–126:
... converte
in bozzacchioni le sosine vere.

Purg. II, 88–89 (L, AKC):
Così com'io t'amai
nel mortal corpo, così t'amo sciolta:

Inf. III, 59 (Whitfield, [1960], 30):
vidi e conobbi l'ombra di colui

Texts Reflecting Passages in Dante

§444:
... un tal figliuolo, ... che gli appartiene meno che a Giuseppo non fece Cristo.

Rime (MM, AKC), LXXVII (Barbi, = LXXIV, Foster & Boyde), 9–11:
E tal giace per lui nel letto tristo,
per tema non sia preso a lo 'mbolare,
che gli appartien quanto Giosepp'a Cristo.

§447:
A così buona vita ... e a così santa ...

Par. XV, 130–131 (L, AKC):
A così riposato, a così bello viver ...

§448:
... ella è tale quale io assai brievemente te la disegnai.

Purg. XXII, 74 (L):
ma perché veggi mei ciò ch'io disegno,

§460:
... matta bestialità ...

Inf. XI, 82–83:
... la matta/bestialitade ...

§469:
Ma se cotale avessi la mente avuta e lo 'ntelletto sano ...

Inf. IX, 61 (TN, AKC):
O voi ch'avete li 'ntelletti sani,

§501:
Ma tu rificchi pur gli occhi della mente ad una cosa, ...

Purg. XV, 64–65 (L, MM, AKC):
Però che tu rificchi
la mente pur a le cose terrene, ...

§503:
Ma non sai tu qual sia la vera gentilezza e quale la falsa? Non sai tu che cosa sia che faccia l'uomo gentile e qual sia quella che gentile esser non lascia?

Conv. IV, i, 7 (L, PGR, MM, AKC):
Questo è l'errore de l'umana bontade in quanto in noi è da la natura seminata e che 'nobilitate' chiamare si dee; che per mala consuetudine e per poco intelletto era tanto fortificato, che l'oppinione, quasi di tutti, n'era falsificata;

§513:
Io aveva con la fronte bassa, sì come coloro che il lor fallo riconoscono, ascoltato ...

Purg. XXXI, 64–66 (L, TN, MM):
Quali fanciulli, vergognando, muti
con li occhi a terra stannosi, ascoltando
e sé riconoscendo e ripentuti,

§514:
... donna della mia mente,

VN II, 1 (AKC):
... la gloriosa donna de la mia mente ...

§515:
... di ciò che mi pareva davanti ora mi pare il contrario;

Par. VIII, 136 (MM):
Or qual che t'era dietro t'è davanti:

§520:
... te sì compunto veggio ...

Inf. I, 15 (PGR, AKC):
che m'avea di paura il cor compunto,

69

Appendix 1

§537:
... mentre nel mortal mondo dimorasti,

§538:
... tutti di carità ardiamo ...

§542:
... per quella pace che per te ardendo s'aspetta, ...

§545:
Mentre lo spirito queste ultime parole diceva, ...

§545:
... a me ... parve levare la testa verso levante ...

§546:
Il quale [lume], poiché in grandissima quantità il cielo ebbe imbiancato, subitamente divenne grandissimo; e senza più verso noi farsi che solamente co' raggi suoi, in quella guisa che noi talvolta veggiamo, tra due oscuri nuvoli trapassando, il sole in terra fare una lunga riga di luce, ...

§547:
... mi parve che non so che cosa grave e ponderosa molto da dosso mi si levasse;

§551:
Mossesi adunque lo spirito, e ... me ... si trasse dietro.

§552:
... quivi il cielo aperto e luminoso per tutto veder mi parve, e sentire l'aere dolce e soave e lieto, e veder le piante verdi e i fiori per le campagne, le quali cose tutto il petto, delle passate noie afflitto, riconfortarono e ritornar nella prima allegrezza.

§553:
... io mi rivolsi indietro a riguardare

Par. XXV, 35 (L):
... che vien qua sù del mortal mondo,

Purg. XV, 57 (L, AKC):
e più di caritate arde ...

Purg. III, 74–75 (L, MM, AKC):
per quella pace
ch'i' credo che per voi tutti s'aspetti,

Inf. V, 139:
Mentre che l'uno spirto questo disse,

Inf. I, 16–18 (L, AKC):
guardai in alto e vidi le sue spalle
vestite già de' raggi del pianeta
che mena dritto altrui per ogne calle.

Par. XXIII, 79–84:
Come a raggio di sol, che puro mei
per fratta nube, già prato di fiori
vider, coverti d'ombra, li occhi miei;
vid' io così più turbe di splendori,
folgorate di sù da raggi ardenti,
sanza veder principio di folgòri

Purg. XII, 118–120 (AKC?):
Maestro, dì, qual cosa greve
levata s'è da me, che nulla quasi
per me fatica, andando, si riceve?

Inf. I, 136:
Allor si mosse, e io li tenni dietro.

Purg. I, 13–18 (L, AKC):
Dolce color d'orïental zaffiro,
che s'accoglieva nel sereno aspetto
del mezzo, puro infino al primo giro,
a li occhi miei ricominciò diletto,
tosto ch'io usci' fuor de l'aura morta
che m'avea contristati li occhi e 'l petto.

Inf. I, 25–26 (L, PGR, MM, AKC):
così l'animo mio, ch'ancor fuggiva,

Texts Reflecting Passages in Dante

il luogo del quale tratto m'avea;

§554:
E avendomi detto me essere libero e potere di me fare a mio senno, . . .

§554:
. . . tanta fu la letizia che io sentii, che vogliendomigli a' piè gittare e grazie rendergli di tanto e tal beneficio,

§554:
. . . esso e il mio sonno ad un' ora si dipartiro.

§555:
. . . tutto di sudore bagnato . . .

§555:
. . . se col vero corpo la montagna salita avessi che nel sogno mi parve salire, . . .

§556:
. . . della misera valle uscire . . .

§559:
. . . se tempo mi fia conceduto, io spero sì con parole gastigare colei, . . .

§561:

. . . ti guarda (piccola mia operetta) di non venire nelle mani delle malvage femmine, e massimamente di colei che ogni demonio di malvagità trapassa e che della presente tua fatica è stata cagione; per ciò che tu saresti là mal ricevuta; ed ella è da pugnere con più aguto stimolo che tu non porti teco.

si volse a retro a rimirar lo passo . . .

Purg. XXVII, 140–142 (MM, AKC):
libero, dritto e sano è tuo arbitrio, e fallo fora non fare a suo senno: per ch'io te sovra te corono e mitrio.

Purg. XXX, 43–46 (L, AKC—citing 49–51):
volsimi a la sinistra col respitto col quale il fantolin corre a la mamma
quando ha paura o quando elli è afflitto,
per dicere a Virgilio: "Men che dramma . . ."

Purg. IX, 63 (AKC):
poi ella e 'l sonno ad una se n'andaro.

Inf. III, 132:
la mente di sudore ancor mi bagna.

Par. I, 73–75:
S'i' era sol di me quel che creasti novellamente, amor che 'l ciel governi,
tu 'l sai, che col tuo lume mi levasti.

Purg. XIV, 4:
. . . la misera valle . . .

VN XLII, 2:
. . . se . . . la mia vita duri per alquanti anni, io spero di dicer di lei quello che mai non fue detto d'alcuna.

Rime (AKC), CIII (Barbi, = LXXX, Foster & Boyde), 79–84:
Canzon, vattene dritto a quella donna
che m'ha ferito il core e che m'invola quello ond'io ho più gola,
e dàlle per lo cor d'una saetta;
ché bell'onor s'acquista in far vendetta.

Appendix 2

THE PROEM OF THE *CORBACCIO*: SOURCES AND ANALOGUES

Indications in brackets [ ] = poses struck by narrator; (AKC) = ascription found in notes to Anthony K. Cassell's translation.

*

§1 [the dutifully grateful recipient]: Qualunque persona, *tacendo*, i *benefìci ricevuti* nasconde senza di ciò aver cagione convenevole, secondo il mio giudicio assai manifestamente dimostra sé essere ingrato e mal conoscente di quelli.

Dec., Pr., 6:
Ma quantunque cessata sia la pena, non per ciò è la memoria fuggita de' *benefici già ricevuti*, . . .

Dec., IV, Intro., 2:
. . . estimava io che lo 'mpetuoso vento e ardente della *'nvidia* non dovesse *percuotere* se non l'alte torri o *le più levate cime* degli alberi: ma io mi truovo della mia estimazione ingannato.
cf. *Par.* XVII, 133–134:
Questo tuo grido farà come vento, che *le più alte cime* più *percuote*;

Par. XVII, 85–99:
"Le sue magnificenze conosciute
  saranno ancora, sì che ' suoi nemici
non ne potran tener *le lingue mute*.
A lui t'aspetta e a' suoi *benefici*;
  per lui fia trasmutata molta gente,
  cambiando condizion ricchi e mendici;
e portera'ne scritto ne la mente
  di lui, e nol dirai"; e disse cose
  incredibili a quei che fier presente.
Poi giunse: "Figlio, queste son le chiose
  di quel che ti fu detto; ecco le insidie
  che dietro a pochi giri son nascose.
Non vo' però ch'a' tuoi vicini *invidie*,
  poscia che s'infutura la tua vita
  via più là che 'l punir di lor perfidie."

*

The Proem: Sources and Analogues

§2 [the offended moralist]: O cosa iniqua e a Dio dispiacevole e gravissima a' discreti uomini, il cui [= ingratitude's] *malvagio fuoco il fonte* secca *della pietà!*

Dec., Conc. Aut., 9:
Chi non sa che il *fuoco* è utilissimo, anzi necessario a' mortali? direm noi, per ciò che egli arde le case e le ville e le città, che sia *malvagio?*

Mon. II, v, 5 & *Ep.* V, 7 (AKC):
"Romanum imperium de *Fonte* nascitur *pietatis.*"
... cum sit Caesar et maiestas eius de *Fonte* defluat *pietatis.*

*

§3 [the humble scribe, aided by a higher authority]: Del quale acciò che niuno mi possa meritamente riprendere, intendo di dimostrare nell'*umile trattato* seguente una speziale *grazia, non per mio merito*, ma per sola *benignità di Colei che impetrandola da Colui che vuol quello ch'ella medesima*, nuovamente mi fu conceduta.

Dec., IV, Intro., 3:
... le presenti novellette ..., le quali non solamente in fiorentin volgare e in prosa scritte per me sono e senza titolo, ma ancora in *istilo umilissimo e rimesso* quanto il più si possono.

cf. *Ep.* XIII, 31:
... ad modum loquendi, *remissus est modus et humilis.*

Dec. Conc. Aut., 1:
Nobilissime giovani ..., io mi credo, aiutantemi la divina grazia ... per li vostri pietosi prieghi *non già per li miei meriti*, quello compiutamente aver fornito che ... promisi di dover fare:

Inf. I, 8:
ma per *trattar* del ben ch'i' vi trovai

Inf. III, 95–96; V, 23–24 (AKC):
vuolsi così colà dove si puote ciò che si vuole, e più non dimandare.

Par. XXXIII, 34–35 (AKC), 36–37:
"Ancor ti priego, regina, *che puoi ciò che tu vuoli*, che conservi sani, dopo tanto veder, li affetti suoi.
Vinca tua guardia i movimenti umani:"

Par. XXXIII, 16 (of Mary):
La tua *benignità* non pur soccorre ...

Par. XXXII, 145–148:
Veramente, *ne* forse tu t'arretri movendo l'ali tue, credendo oltrarti, *orando grazia conven che s'impetri* grazia da quella che puote aiutarti;

*

§4 [the helper of humankind]: La qual cosa faccendo, non solamente *parte del mio dovere pagherò*, ma sanza niuno dubbio potrò a molti *lettori* di quella fare *utilità.*

Purg. X, 106–108:
Non vo' però, *lettor*, che tu ti smaghi

Appendix 2

Dec., Pr., 8:
E quantunque il mio sostentamento
... possa essere ..., nondimeno
parmi quello doversi più tosto por-
gere dove il bisogno apparisce maggiore, sì perché più *utilità* vi farà. ...

Dec., Conc. Aut., 14:
Chi vorrà da quelle malvagio consiglio e malvagia operazione trarre,
elle nol vieteranno a alcuno ....: e chi
utilità e frutto ne vorrà, elle nol
negheranno. ...

di buon proponimento per udire
come Dio vuol che 'l *debito si paghi*.

*

§5 [the invoker of divine assistance on behalf of others]: E perciò, acciò che
questo ne segua, divotamente priego Colui del quale e quello di che io debbo
dire e ogni altro bene procedette e procede, e che di tutti, come per effetto si
vede, è larghissimo donatore, che alla presente opera della sua luce siffattamente *illumini il mio intelletto* e la *mano* scrivente regga, che per me quello si
scriva che onore e gloria sia del suo santissimo nome, *e utilità e consolazione*
delle anime di coloro *li quali* per avventura ciò *leggeranno*, e altro no.

Dec., Conc. Aut., 1:
... a *consolazion* delle quali [nobil-
issime giovani] io a così lunga fatica
messo mi sono, ... per la qual cosa
[completing the *Dec.*] Idio primiera-
mente e appresso voi ringraziando, è
da dare alla penna e alla *man* faticata
riposo.

Dec., Pr., 14:
... delle quali [novelle] le già dette
donne, che *queste leggeranno*, pari-
mente *diletto* della sollazzevoli cose in
quelle mostrate e *utile consiglio* potranno pigliare, in quanto potranno
cognoscere quello che sia da fuggire
e che sia similmente da seguitare.

Dec. Conc. Aut., 14:
... né sarà mai che altro che *utile e*
oneste sien dette o tenute, se a que'
tempi o a quelle persone *si leggeranno*
per cui e pe' quali state son
raccontate.

Par. IV, 124–126:
Io veggio bene che già mai non si
sazia
nostro intelletto, se 'l ver non lo
illustra
di fuor dal qual nessun vero si
spazia.

*

The Proem: Sources and Analogues

There are . . . frequent similarities between the positions taken by the narrators of the *Decameron* and the *Corbaccio*. Both have recently been freed from their imprisonment in love by a *consolatore*—the unnamed friend of the *Decameron* with "le sue laudevoli consolazioni" (*Pr.* 4) and the *pensiero*, "credo da celeste lume mandato" (12) that brings down "divina consolazione nelle menti de' mortali" (47). Each narrator was about to die because of his amorous disposition (*Pr.* 4; *Corb.* 9). Each thanks God for His mercy (*Pr.* 5; *Corb.* 4), and now wishes to express his gratitude for "benefici ricevuti" (*Pr.* 6; *Corb.* 1) so as not to seem "ingrato" (*Pr.* 7; *Corb.* 1). Each hopes that his work will offer *utilità* to its intended readership (*Pr.* 8; *Corb.* 4). Where that readership is feminine in one case and masculine in another, both the lovestruck ladies for whom the narrator of the *Decameron* feels the compassion of fellowship and the formerly love-struck narrator of the *Corbaccio* are seen as being or having been confined to their quarters by their maladies ("nel piccolo circuito delle loro camere racchiuse dimorano"—*Pr.* 10; "ritrovandom'io solo nella mia camera"—*Corb.* 6). And both works have as their aims solace and utility: "diletto delle sollazzevoli cose in quelle mostrate e utile consiglio potranno pigliare" (*Pr.* 14); "utilità e consolazione delle anime" (*Corb.* 5). (*Boccaccio's Two Venuses* [1977], 141–42)

Appendix 3

A PARTIAL CENSUS OF SOME CRITICAL VIEWS CONCERNING VARIOUS PROBLEMS IN THE *CORBACCIO*

TEXT IS AUTOBIOGRAPHICAL	A "FABULA"
Manni (1742), p. 75	
Crescini (1887)	
Dobelli (1898), p. 269	
Hauvette (1901)	Billanovich (1947)
Padoan (1963), p. 11n.	Lopriore (1956)
Cottino-Jones (1970), p. 490	Whitfield (1960), p. 31
Leone (1973)	Cassell (1975)
Cartier (1975), pp. 339–48	Marti (1976), pp. 71–74
Hastings (1975), p. 24n.	Nurmela (1977), pp. 194–96
Bergin (1981), pp. 199–200	Bragantini (1981–82), p. 199

BOCCACCIO IS SERIOUS	JOKING
Lopriore (1956)	
Bruni (1974 & 1977)	Cassell (1974), p. 70 (almost)
Almansi (1975), pp. 93, 154	Barricelli (1975)
Cartier (1975)	
Marti (1976), pp. 75–83	
Nurmela (1977)	
Nepaulsingh (1980)	
Bergin (1981)	
Marcus (1984)	
Mazzotta (1986), p. 74	Nykrog (1984)

Census of Critical Views

DATE: WRITTEN 1354–55	1365–66
traditional view, dating from Manni (1742), p. 75, citing §179	Padoan (1963) many accept (see Padoan [1978], p. 199) but debate is joined:
those not convinced by Padoan: Ricci (1965), p. 1271 Nurmela (1968) Zaccaria (1969), pp. 339–40 Bruni (1974), p. 162n. Cartier (1975), p. 340–43 Cassell (1975) Hollander (1977), p. 139 Bergin (1981), pp. 190–91 Iovino (1983), pp. 35–37 Kirkham (1985), p. 338 Smarr (1986), p. 149	*those convinced:* Branca (1967), p. 140 Cottino-Jones (1970), p. 507 Barricelli (1975), p. 95 Marti (1976), pp. 63–71, (accepts Padoan's revised dating if with some adjustments) Padoan (1978) accepts Marti's arguments for date of 1363–66
CITATIONS OF DANTE SERIOUS	PARODIC
Cavallari (1921), pp. 441–44 Marti (1976), pp. 74–75	Burich (1941), pp. 45–46 Cassell (1974 & 1975) Barricelli (1975), pp. 105–07 Nykrog (1984), p. 439

REMEDIA AMORIS AS SOURCE

Billanovich (1947), pp. 161–62
Padoan (1963), p. 11n.
Bruni (1974): *De vetula*
Cassell (1974), p. 68
Nardo (1979): *Ars amatoria*
Smarr (1986), pp. 155–56, 162–63

TITLE REFERS TO WIDOW (SEE ROSSI [1962] AND ZACCARIA [1969] FOR REVIEW OF INTERPRETATIONS)

Padoan (1963), pp. 19n., 200–01
Cassell (1970)
Cottino-Jones (1970), p. 502
Cartier (1975), pp. 337–39
Marti (1976), pp. 60–62
Bergin (1981), p. 191

Appendix 4:

THE *REMEDIA AMORIS* AND THE *PROEMIO* OF THE *DECAMERON*

1. The narrators as past and present lovers:

    > ego semper amavi,
    > Et si, quid faciam nunc quoque, quaeris, amo (7–8).

    > ... dalla mia prima giovanezza infino a questo tempo oltre modo essendo acceso stato d'altissimo e nobile amore . . .; mi fu egli di grandissima fatica a sofferire, certo non per crudeltà della donna amata, ma per soverchio fuoco nella mente concetto da poco regolato appetito (3). . . . il mio amore . . . si diminuì in guisa, che sol di se nella mente m'ha al presente lasciato quel piacere che egli è usato di porgere a chi troppo non si mette ne' suoi più cupi pelaghi navigando; per che, dove faticoso esser solea, ogni affanno togliendo via, dilettevole il sento esser rimaso (5).

2. Unhappy love as leading to death:

    > At siquis male fert indignae regna puellae,
    > Ne pereat, nostrae sentiat artis opem (15–16).

    > Qui, nisi desierit, misero periturus amore est,
    > Desinat . . . (21–22).

    > Nella qual noia tanto rifrigerio già mi porsero i piacevoli ragionamenti d'alcuno amico e le sue laudevoli consolazioni, che io porto fermissima opinione per quelle essere avenuto che io non sia morto (4).

3. The need to be free of Love's sway:

    > Publicus assertor dominis suppressa levabo
    > Pectora: vindictae quisque favete suae (73–74).

    > Optimus ille sui vindex, laedentia pectus
    > Vincula qui rupit, dedoluitque semel (293–294).

The Remedia Amoris *and the* Proemio

> . . . ora che libero dir mi posso . . . (7).

> . . . a Amore [le donne] ne rendano grazie, il quale liberandomi da' suoi legami m'ha conceduto il potere attendere a' lor piaceri (15).

4. *Otium* as cause of unhappy love:

> . . . fugias otia prima . . . (136).

> Otia si tollas, periere Cupidinis arcus . . . (139).

> Tam Venus otia amat; qui finem quaeris amoris,
>   Cedit amor rebus: res age, tutus eris (143–144).

> Esse dentro a' dilicati petti, temendo e vergognando, tengono l'amorose fiamme nascose [cf. *Rem.* 105: "tacitae serpunt in viscera flammae"] . . . , e oltre a ciò . . . il più del tempo nel piccolo circuito delle loro camere racchiuse dimorano e quasi oziose sedendosi . . . (10).

5. Activities which counteract lovesickness:

> Rura quoque oblectant animos . . . (169)

> . . . tu venandi studium cole . . . (199)

> Lenius est studium, studium tamen, alite capta
>   Aut lino aut calamis praemia parva sequi,
> Vel, quae piscis edax avido male devoret ore,
>   Abdere suspensis aera recurva cibis (207–210).

> [Gli uomini], se alcuna malinconia o gravezza di pensieri gli affligge, hanno molti modi da allaggiare o da passar quello . . . ; volendo essi, non manca l'andare a torno, udire e veder molte cose, uccellare, cacciare, pescare, cavalcare, giucare o mercatare (12).

6. Author's advice on what to flee, what to seek:

> . . . quos [cibos] fugias quosque sequare, dabo (796).

> . . . parimente diletto delle sollazzevoli cose in quelle [novelle] mostrate e utile consiglio potranno [le donne] pigliare, in quanto potranno cognoscere quello che sia da fuggire e che sia similmente da seguitare (14).

7. Both authors conclude in a similar vein (indicating the thanks due them from their auditors):

> Postmodo reddetis sacro pia vota poetae,
>   Carmine sanati femina virque meo (813–814).

> Il che [passamento di noia] se avviene, che voglia Idio che così sia, a Amore ne rendano grazie, il quale liberandomi da' suoi legami m'ha conceduto il potere attendere a' lor piaceri (15).

BIBLIOGRAPHY

Almansi, Guido. "Alcune osservazioni sulla novella dello scolaro e della vedova," *Studi sul Boccaccio* 8 (1974):137-45.
———. *The Writer as Liar*. London & Boston: Routledge & Kegan Paul, 1975.
Barolini, Teodolinda. "Giovanni Boccaccio." In *European Writers: The Middle Ages and the Renaissance*, ed. W. T. H. Jackson. New York: Charles Scribner's Sons, 1983, 530.
Barricelli, Gian Piero. "Satire of Satire: Boccaccio's *Corbaccio*." *Italian Quarterly* 18 (1975):95-111.
Battaglia, Salvatore. "Elementi autobiografici nell'arte del Boccaccio." *La Cultura* 9 (1930):241-54. Reprinted in his *Giovanni Boccaccio e la riforma della narrativa*. Naples: Liguori, 1969, 119-34.
———. "La tradizione di Ovidio nel medioevo." In his *La Coscienza letteraria del medioevo*. Naples: Liguori, 1965, 23-50.
Bergin, Thomas G. *Boccaccio*. New York: Viking, 1981, 190-203.
Bettinzoli, Attilio. "Per una definizione delle presenze dantesche nel *Decameron*: 1. I registri 'ideologici', lirici, drammatici." *Studi sul Boccaccio* 13 (1981-82): 267-326.
Billanovich, Giuseppe, "Le fondamenta del *Decameron*: il *Corbaccio*, favola-trattato." In his *Restauri boccacceschi*. Rome: Edizioni di "Storia e letteratura," 1947, 131-63.
Bourciez, Jean. "Sur l'énigme du *Corbaccio*." *Revue des langues romanes* 72 (1957-58):330-37.
Bragantini, Renzo. "Dall'allegoria all'immagine. Durata e metamorfosi di un tema (per la novella VIII 7 del *Decameron*)." *Studi sul Boccaccio* 13 (1981-82): 199-216.
Branca, Vittore. *Tradizione delle opere di Giovanni Boccaccio*. Rome: Edizioni di "Storia e letteratura," 1958, 24-29.
———. "Profilo biografico." *Tutte le opere di Giovanni Boccaccio* 1. Milan: Mondadori, 1967, 3-203.
———. and Pier Giorgio Ricci. "Notizie e documenti per la biografia del Boccaccio." *Studi sul Boccaccio* 5 (1969):1-18.
Brown, Margery L. "The *Hous of Fame* and the *Corbaccio*." *MLN* 22 (1917): 411-15.
Bruni, Francesco. "Dal *De vetula* al *Corbaccio*: l'idea d'amore e i due tempi dell'intellettuale." *Medioevo romanzo* 1, no. 2 (1974):161-216.
———. "*Historia Calamitatum, Secretum, Corbaccio*: tre posizioni su *luxuria (-amor)*

Bibliography

e *superbia (-gloria)."* In *Boccaccio in Europe: Proceedings of the Boccaccio Conference, Louvain, December 1975,* ed. G. Tournoy. Louvain: Leuven University Press, 1977, 23–52.

Burich, Enrico. "Boccaccio und Dante." *Deutsches Dante-Jahrbuch* 23 (1941): 36–59.

Cartier, Normand R. "Boccaccio's Old Crow." *Romania* 98 (1975): 331–48.

Cassell, Anthony K. "The Crow of the Fable and the *Corbaccio:* A Suggestion for the Title." *MLN* 85 (1970):83–91.

———. "*Il Corbaccio* and the Secundus Tradition." *Comparative Literature* 25 (1973): 352–60.

———. "An Abandoned Canvas: Structural and Moral Conflict in the *Corbaccio.*" *MLN* 89 (1974): 60–70.

———. trans. *The Corbaccio.* Urbana: University of Illinois Press, 1975.

Cavallari, Elisabetta. *La fortuna di Dante nel Trecento.* Florence: F. Perella, 1921, 441–44.

Cioffari, Vincenzo. "The Function of Fortune in Dante, Boccaccio and Machiavelli." *Italica* 24 (1947):1–13.

Cottino-Jones, Marga. "The *Corbaccio:* Notes for a Mythical Perspective of Moral Alternatives." *Forum Italicum* 4, no. 4 (1970):490–509.

Crescini, Vincenzo. *Contributo agli studi sul Boccaccio.* Turin: E. Loescher, 1887.

De Gubernatis, Angelo. *Giovanni Boccaccio: Corso di lezioni fatte nell'Università di Roma nell'anno 1904–1905.* Milan: Editrice Lombarda, n.d., 427–48.

Delcorno, Carlo. "Note sui dantismi nell' *Elegia di Madonna Fiammetta.*" *Studi sul Boccaccio* 11 (1979):251–94.

Della Torre, Arnaldo. *La giovinezza di Giovanni Boccaccio.* Città di Castello: Lapi, 1905.

Dobelli, Ausonio. "Il culto del Boccaccio per Dante." *Giornale dantesco* 5 (1898): 267–69.

Hastings, Robert. *Nature and Reason in the "Decameron."* Publications of the Faculty of Arts and Letters of the University of Manchester, no. 21. Manchester: Manchester University Press, 1975.

Hauvette, Henri. "Une confession de Boccace: *Il Corbaccio.*" *Bulletin italien* 1 (1901):3–21.

———. *Boccace, étude biographique et littéraire.* Paris: A. Colin, 1914.

Hollander, Robert. *Boccaccio's Two Venuses.* New York: Columbia University Press, 1977.

———. "Boccaccio's Dante: Imitative Distance (*Decameron* 1.1 and 6.10)." *Studi sul Boccaccio* 13 (1981–82): 169–98.

———. "«Utilità» in Boccaccio's *Decameron.*" *Studi sul Boccaccio* 15 (1985–86): 215–33.

Iovino, Angela M. "The *Decameron* and the *Corbaccio:* Boccaccio's Image of Women and Spiritual Crisis." Ph.D. diss., Indiana University, 1983.

Jeffery, Violet M. "Boccaccio's Titles and the Meaning of the *Corbaccio.*" *Modern Language Review* 28 (1933): 194–204.

Kirkham, Victoria. "Boccaccio's Dedication to Women in Love." In *Renaissance Studies in Honor of Craig Hugh Smyth* 1. Florence: Giunti Barbèra, 1985, 333–43.

Koerting, Gustav. *Boccaccios Leben und Werke.* Leipzig: R. Reisland, 1880.

Landau, Marcus. *Giovanni Boccaccio, sein Leben und seine Werke.* Stuttgart: J. G.

Bibliography

Cotta, 1877. Italian trans., C. Antona-Traversi, *Giovanni Boccaccio, sua vita e sue opere*. Naples: Stamperia del Vaglio, 1881–82.

Leone, Michael. "Tra autobiografismo reale e ideale in *Decameron* VIII, 7." *Italica* 50 (1973): 242–65.

Levi, Attilio. *"Il Corbaccio" e "La Divina Commedia."* Turin: E. Loescher, 1889.

Lopriore, Giuseppe Italo. "Osservazioni sul *Corbaccio*." *Rassegna della letteratura italiana* 60 (1956): 483–89.

Luchaire, Lucien. *Boccace*. Paris: Flammarion, 1951.

Macrì-Leone, Francesco. "La politica di Giovanni Boccaccio." *Giornale storico della letteratura italiana* 15 (1890): 79–110.

Manni, Domenico Maria. *Istoria del "Decamerone" di Giovanni Boccaccio*. Florence: A. Ristori, 1742.

Marcus, Millicent. "Misogyny as Misreading: A Gloss on *Decameron* VIII, 7." *Stanford Italian Review* 4 (Spring 1984): 23–40.

Marti, Mario, ed. *Opere minori in volgare di Giovanni Boccaccio*. Vol. 4. Milan: Rizzoli, 1972, 201–308.

———. "Per una metalettura del *Corbaccio*: il ripudio di Fiammetta." *Giornale storico della letteratura italiana* 153 (1976): 60–86.

Mazzotta, Giuseppe. *The World at Play in Boccaccio's "Decameron."* Princeton: Princeton University Press, 1986.

Muscetta, Carlo. *Giovanni Boccaccio*. Bari: Laterza, 1972.

Nardo, Dante. "Sulle fonti classiche del *Corbaccio*." *Medioevo e umanesimo* 34 (1979): 245–54 (= *Medioevo e rinascimento veneto con altri studi in onore di Lino Lazzarini*, vol. 1).

Nepaulsingh, Colbert I. "Juan Ruiz, Boccaccio, and the Antifeminist Tradition." *La Corònica* 9 (1980): 13–18.

Nurmela, Tauno. "Manuscrits et éditions du *Corbaccio* de Boccace." *Neuphilologische Mitteilungen* 54 (1953): 102–34.

———. "Études critiques sur le texte du *Corbaccio* de Boccace." *Mémoires de la Societé Néophilologique de Helsinki* 25 (1963): 5–53.

———. "Il testo del *Corbaccio* e il codice di Mannelli." *Primo Congresso degli Italianisti Scandinavi: Atti* s. 1. Stockholm, May 20–22, 1963. Ed. S. Ponzanello and D. Ghio, 1965.

———. ed. *Il Corbaccio*, Suomalaisen Tiedeakatemian Toimituksia: Annales Academiae Scientiarum Fennicae. Ser. B, 147. Helsinki, 1968.

———. "Sulle tracce di Boccaccio." *Il Veltro* 19 (1975): 605–08.

———. "La misogynie chez Boccace." In *Boccaccio in Europe: Proceedings of the Boccaccio Conference, Louvain, December 1975*, ed. G. Tournoy. Louvain: Leuven University Press, 1977, 191–96.

Nykrog, Per. "Playing Games with Fiction: *Les Quinze Joyes de Mariage, Il Corbaccio, El Arcipreste de Talavera*." In *The Craft of Fiction: Essays in Medieval Poetics*, ed. Leigh A. Arrathoon. Rochester, Mich.: Solaris Press, 1984, 436–41.

Ó Cuilleanáin, Cormac. *Religion and the Clergy in Boccaccio's "Decameron."* Rome: Edizioni di storia e letteratura (Letture di pensiero e d'arte), 1984.

Padoan, Giorgio. "Sulla datazione del *Corbaccio*." In his *Il Boccaccio, le muse, il Parnaso e l'Arno*. Florence: Olschki, 1978, 199–228. (*Lettere Italiane* 15 [1963]: 1–27, 199–201.)

———. "Mondo aristocratico e mondo comunale nell'ideologia e nell'arte di

Giovanni Boccaccio." Ibid., 1–91. (First in *Studi sul Boccaccio* 2 [1964]:81–216.)
Pinelli, Giovanni. "Appunti sul *Corbaccio*." *Il Propugnatore* 16 (1883): 162–92.
Rajna, Pio. "Il libro di Andrea Capellano in Italia nei secoli XIII e XIV." *Studi di filologia romanza* 5 (1891):205–24.
Ricci, Pier Giorgio. "Studi sulle opere latine e volgari del Boccaccio." *Rinascimento* 10 (1959):3–32; n.s. 2 (1962):20–29.
———. ed. *Giovanni Boccaccio, Opere in versi, Corbaccio, Trattatello in laude di Dante, Prose latine, Epistole*. La letteratura italiana: Storia e Testi, 9. Milan–Naples: R. Ricciardi, 1965.
———. "Notizie e documenti per la biografia del Boccaccio." *Studi sul Boccaccio* 6 (1971):1–10.
Romano, David. "L'edizione (1498) ed i codici del *Corbaccio* catalano." *Studi sul Boccaccio* 11 (1979):413–19.
Rossi, Aldo. "Proposta per un titolo del Boccaccio: *Il Corbaccio*." *Studi di filologia italiana* 20 (1962):383–90.
Sapegno, Natalino. *Il Trecento*. Milan: F. Vallardi, 1938, 366–70.
Scaglione, Aldo D. *Nature and Love in the Late Middle Ages: An Essay on the Cultural Context of the "Decameron."* Berkeley and Los Angeles: University of California Press, 1963.
Smarr, Janet Levarie. *Boccaccio and Fiammetta*. Urbana and Chicago: University of Illinois Press, 1986, 149–64.
Symonds, John Addington. *Giovanni Boccaccio as Man and Author*. New York: Scribner's, 1895.
Torraca, Francesco. *Per la biografia di Giovanni Boccaccio*. Rome: Società editrice Dante Alighieri, 1912.
Tripet, Arnaud. "Boccace et son clerc amoureux." *Bibliothèque d'humanisme et renaissance* 29, no. 1 (1967):7–20.
Ussani, Jr., Vincenzo. "Alcune imitazioni ovidiane del Boccaccio." *Maia* 1 (1948): 289–306.
Varanini, Giorgio. "La *Canzone dello indovinello*." *Studi e problemi di critica testuale* 4 (1972):26–33.
Watson, Paul F. "An Immodest Proposal, Concerning the *Corbaccio*." *Studi sul Boccaccio* 16 (1987–88) [forthcoming].
Whitfield, J. H. "Dante in Boccaccio." *Italian Studies* 15 (1960), supplement [The Barlow Lectures on Dante, 1959, 2]:16–32.
Wilkins, Ernest Hatch. "The Date of Birth of Boccaccio." *Romanic Review* 4 (1910):369.
Zaccaria, Vittorio. "G. Boccaccio, *Il Corbaccio* . . . a cura di T. Nurmela" (review article). *Studi sul Boccaccio* 5 (1969):331–40.

INDEX OF WORKS
AND AUTHORS CITED

Andreas Capellanus, *28; 46; 48*
Aristotle, *46*
Augustine, *23*

Barricelli, G. P., *1; 3; 26; 42; 45; 46; 52*
Bartoli, L., *49*
Benvenuto da Imola, *46*
Bergin, T. G., *50*
Bettinzoli, A., *51; 52; 57*
Bible, Romans 12:19, *9*
Billanovich, Gius., *27; 29; 42; 56*
Billanovich, Guido, *55*
Boccaccio, *Amorosa Visione, 19; 24; 41; 43; 52*
  Caccia di Diana, 23; 54
  Comedia delle ninfe, 19; 25; 52
  Consolatoria a Pino de' Rossi, 31
  Decameron, 9; 26; 28; 29; 30; 32; 33; 38; 39; 41; 43; 46; 53; 55; 56
  Decameron (as companion to *Corbaccio*), *1; 28; 33; 50; 53;* (as "Galleotto"), *34*
    Proemio, *6; 29; 36; 39; 43; 46; 49; 51; 56; 57; 78–79*
    I, Intro., 8, *53*
    I, Intro., 49, 51, *50*
    IV, Intro., *43*
    IV, Intro., 2–4, *57*
    IV, Intro., 5, *57*
    IV, Intro., 33–34, *30*
    VII, *50*
    VII, Conc., 3, 22; *50*
    VIII, *50*
    VIII, vii, *1; 29; 31; 32; 51; 52; 18–23*
    IX, x, 3, *54*
    X, Conc. Aut., *43*
    X, Conc. Aut., 3, *57*
    rubrics, *50*

Elegia di madonna Fiammetta, 3; 19; 23; 40
Esposizioni, 30; Inf. IV, esp. litt., 122, *55; Inf.* IV, esp. litt., 237, *47; Inf.* VII, esp. all., 111, *46; Inf.* XIII, 151, *56; Inf.* XVI, esp. litt., 27–46, *54*
Filocolo, 19; 25; 53
Filostrato, 3; 19
Genealogia, 30
Latin works, *25*
Ninfale fiesolano, 25
Teseida, 19
Boethius, *2; 5; 6; 8; 9; 16; 47*
Branca, V., *20; 29; 30; 33; 50; 52; 53*
Brownlee, M. S., *40*

Callimachus, *34; 38; 55*
Cartier, N. R., *54*
Cassell, A. K., *3; 17; 26; 46; 48; 49; 50; 51; 53; 54; 56*
Castelvetro, L., *51*
Cervantes, *55*
Chaucer, G., *24*
Conte, G. B., *58*
Cottino-Jones, M., *54*
Crescini, V., *24*

D'Andrea, A., *50*
Dante, *1; 2; 3; 9; 10; 16; 23; 24; 30; 40–42; 43; 45; 46; 47; 49; 50; 53; 54; 57; 59–74; 77*
De vulg. Eloq., 57
Inf., 5, *9;* I, 52–53, *58;* III, 132, *58;* V, 29, *10;* V, 35, *10;* V, 64, *50;* XII, 137, *52;* XIII, 26, *9;* XXII, 109, *51; Purg.* I, 30–36, *47;* I, 43, *58;* I, 85, *20;* XI, 37, *46;* XIV, 41, *22;*

85

Index

Dante (continued)
 XIV, 42, *22;* XIV, 46, *22;* XIV,
 82-84, *22;* XIV, 88-89, *52;* XIX,
 34-35, *47;* XXVII, 4, *52;* XXX,
 49; XXX, 34-35, *58;* XXX, 55, *47*
Par. I, 73-75, *40;* VIII, 2, *6;* XXI,
 77-78, *58*
Io son venuto (Rime, 100), *51; Così nel mio parlar (Rime,* 103), *17; 51*
V.N., 42; 47; 49-50; XIV, *46;* XLI, *8;*
 XLII, 2, *58*
De Gubernatis, A., *24*
Delcorno, C., *40; 57*
Dolce, L., *50*
Durling, R. M., *51*

Fior di virtù, 55
Flaubert, G., *23*
Forcione, A., *55*
Foscolo, U., *53*
Frankel, M., *58*

Geremia da Montagnone, *55*
Groto, L., *50*
Gybbon-Monypenny, G. B., *48*

Hankey, A. T., *55*
Hastings, R., *52*
Hexter, R. J., *57*
Hollander, R., *23; 24; 26; 33; 34; 42; 46; 47; 50; 51; 52; 53; 54; 56; 57; 58; 75*
Homer, *38*
Horace, *51*

Iovino, A. M., *45; 46; 48; 53; 54*

Jerome, St., *48; 54*
Juvenal, *39; 48; 51; 56*

Kallendorf, C., *49*
Kirkham, V., *23; 46*

Levi, A., *57*
Lopriore, G. I., *50*
Lovato Lovati, *55*

Manni, D. M., *27; 42; 52; 53*
Marcus, M., *18; 21; 51; 52*
Marti, M., *28; 30; 31; 47; 52; 53; 54*
Mozley, J. H., *55*
Mussato, A., *55*

Nardo, D., *56*
Nurmela, T., *2; 9; 27; 28; 48; 54; 56*
Nykrog, P., *3; 56; 58; 45-46*

Ovid, *1; 28; 33; 43; 52; 56; 57*
 Amores, 37; 57
 Ars amatoria, 37; 39; 77
 Ibis, 34-35; 55; 57
 Metamorphoses 2.531-632, *54-55*
 Remedia amoris, 29; 35-39; 43; 46; 57; 77; 78-79
 Remedia amoris, 1, *57;* 655-58, *50;* 796, *56;* 797-98, *56*
Ovid (pseudo-), *De vetula, 77*

Padoan, G., *26-33; 50; 52; 53; 54; 55; 56; 57*
Paul, St., Romans 12:19, *9*
Petrarch, *39; 43*
Pico della Mirandola, *13*
Pinelli, G., *50; 56*

Roman de la rose, 48
Rossi, E., *50*

Sansovino, F., *50*
Smarr, J., *46; 56*

Talavera, *46*
Theophrastus, *48; 54*
Thomas Aquinas, *46*

Virgil, *38; 56; 57*

Watson, P., *34; 55*
Weiss, R., *55*

Zoilus, *38*

86

University of Pennsylvania Press
MIDDLE AGES SERIES
EDWARD PETERS, General Editor

Edward Peters, ed. *Christian Society and the Crusades, 1198–1229.* Sources in Translation, including The Capture of Damietta by Oliver of Paderborn. 1971
Edward Peters, ed. *The First Crusade: The Chronicle of Fulcher of Chartres and Other Source Materials.* 1971
Katherine Fischer Drew, trans. *The Burgundian Code: The Book of Constitutions or Law of Gundobad and Additional Enactments.* 1972
G. G. Coulton. *From St. Francis to Dante: Translations from the Chronicle of the Franciscan Salimbene (1221–1288).* 1972
Alan C. Kors and Edward Peters, eds. *Witchcraft in Europe, 1110–1700: A Documentary History.* 1972
Richard C. Dales. *The Scientific Achievement of the Middle Ages.* 1973
Katherine Fischer Drew, trans. *The Lombard Laws.* 1973
Henry Charles Lea. *The Ordeal.* Part III of Superstition and Force. 1973
Henry Charles Lea. *Torture.* Part IV of Superstition and Force. 1973
Henry Charles Lea (Edward Peters, ed.). *The Duel and the Oath.* Parts I and II of Superstition and Force. 1974
Edward Peters, ed. *Monks, Bishops, and Pagans: Christian Culture in Gaul and Italy, 500–700.* 1975
Jeanne Krochalis and Edward Peters, ed. and trans. *The World of Piers Plowman.* 1975
Julius Goebel, Jr. *Felony and Misdemeanor: A Study in the History of Criminal Law.* 1976
Susan Mosher Stuard, ed. *Women in Medieval Society.* 1976
James Muldoon, ed. *The Expansion of Europe: The First Phase.* 1977
Clifford Peterson. *Saint Erkenwald.* 1977
Robert Somerville and Kenneth Pennington, eds. *Law, Church, and Society: Essays in Honor of Stephan Kuttner.* 1977
Donald E. Queller. *The Fourth Crusade: The Conquest of Constantinople, 1201–1204.* 1977
Pierre Riché (Jo Ann McNamara, trans.). *Daily Life in the World of Charlemagne.* 1978
Charles R. Young. *The Royal Forests of Medieval England.* 1979
Edward Peters, ed. *Heresy and Authority in Medieval Europe.* 1980
Suzanne Fonay Wemple. *Women in Frankish Society: Marriage and the Cloister, 500–900.* 1981
R. G. Davies and J. H. Denton, eds. *The English Parliament in the Middle Ages.* 1981
Edward Peters. *The Magician, the Witch, and the Law.* 1982
Barbara H. Rosenwein. *Rhinoceros Bound: Cluny in the Tenth Century.* 1982

Steven D. Sargent, ed. and trans. *On the Threshold of Exact Science: Selected Writings of Anneliese Maier on Late Medieval Natural Philosophy.* 1982
Benedicta Ward. *Miracles and the Medieval Mind: Theory, Record, and Event, 1000–1215.* 1982
Harry Turtledove, trans. *The Chronicle of Theophanes: An English Translation of* anni mundi *6095–6305 (A.D. 602–813).* 1982
Leonard Cantor, ed. *The English Medieval Landscape.* 1982
Charles T. Davis. *Dante's Italy and Other Essays.* 1984
George T. Dennis, trans. *Maurice's Strategikon: Handbook of Byzantine Military Strategy.* 1984
Thomas F. X. Noble. *The Republic of St. Peter: The Birth of the Papal State, 680–825.* 1984
Kenneth Pennington. *Pope and Bishops: The Papal Monarchy in the Twelfth and Thirteenth Centuries.* 1984
Patrick J. Geary. *Aristocracy in Provence: The Rhône Basin at the Dawn of the Carolingian Age.* 1985
C. Stephen Jaeger. *The Origins of Courtliness: Civilizing Trends and the Formation of Courtly Ideals, 939–1210.* 1985
J. N. Hillgarth, ed. *Christianity and Paganism, 350–750: The Conversion of Western Europe.* 1986
William Chester Jordan. *From Servitude to Freedom: Manumission in the Sénonais in the Thirteenth Century.* 1986
James William Brodman. *Ransoming Captives in Crusader Spain: The Order of Merced on the Christian-Islamic Frontier.* 1986
Frank Tobin. *Meister Eckhart: Thought and Language.* 1986
Daniel Bornstein, trans. *Dino Compagni's Chronicle of Florence.* 1986
James M. Powell. *Anatomy of a Crusade, 1213–1221.* 1986
Jonathan Riley-Smith. *The First Crusade and the Idea of Crusading.* 1986
Susan Mosher Stuard, ed. *Women in Medieval History and Historiography.* 1987
Avril Henry, ed. *The Mirour of Mans Saluacioune.* 1987
María Rosa Menocal. *The Arabic Role in Medieval Literary History.* 1987
Margaret J. Ehrhart. *The Judgment of the Trojan Prince Paris in Medieval Literature.* 1987
Betsy Bowden. *Chaucer Aloud: The Varieties of Textual Interpretation.* 1987
Felipe Fernández-Armesto. *Before Columbus: Exploration and Colonization from the Mediterranean to the Atlantic, 1229–1492.* 1987
Michael Resler, trans. *EREC by Hartmann von Aue.* 1987
A. J. Minnis. *Medieval Theory of Authorship.* 1987
Uta-Renate Blumenthal. *The Investiture Controversy.* 1988
Robert Hollander. *Boccaccio's Last Fiction: "Il Corbaccio."* 1988
Ralph Turner. *Men Raised from the Dust: Administrative Service and Upward Mobility in Angevin England.* 1988
David Anderson. *Before the Knight's Tale: Imitation of Classical Epic in Boccaccio's "Teseida."* 1988
Charlotte A. Newman. *The Anglo-Norman Nobility in the Reign of Henry I.* 1988
Joseph F. O'Callaghan. *The Cortes of Castile-León, 1188–1350.* 1988